Quick Steps To

Direct Selling Success

GARY SPIRER

NEW YORK

Quick Steps To Direct Selling Success

Gary Spirer
© 2011 Gary Spirer. All rights reserved.

ISBN 978-1-60037-820-1 (paperback)

Library of Congress Control Number: 2010932580

Published by:
MORGAN JAMES PUBLISHING
1225 Franklin Ave. Ste 325
Garden City, NY 11530-1693
Toll Free 800-485-4943
www.MorganJamesPublishing.com

Interior Design by:
Bonnie Bushman
bbushman@bresnan.net

Dedication

To Gloria Spirer my mother. Kaisa Kokkonen. Danielle and Alexandra for their ongoing love and support.

Acknowledgments

I would like to acknowledge my family and close friends for supporting and encouraging me to follow my dream and passion of writing and teaching. I want to thank my daughter Danielle for assisting me in the research and editing. I want to thank Kaisa Kokkonen for her valuable input and a continual support and encouragement. Jimmy Smith for his inspiring story and information. Hank Winchester for introducing me to Jimmy Smith and being a loyal friend and business associate. Barbara and Ed Ennis for their guidance and feedback. John Paine for his superb editing. Mark Steisel for his additional excellent editorial work. Ethan Friedman of Level Five Media, my literary agent. Rick Frishman and David Hancock of Morgan James. My daughter Alexandra for her constant typing of redrafts and valued input.

About The Author

GARY SPIRER has spent the past 30 years in the upper echelons of business. In his illustrious career, he has been involved in various aspects of business including real estate, investment banking, publishing, teaching and entertainment. Gary is both a student of business and a practitioner, who has made millions of dollars in a variety of business ventures. Gary also knows and has worked with many leading business figures throughout the world.

Gary began his distinguished career at Lazard Frères, the prestigious investment-banking firm, and then went on to found his real estate company, Capital Hill Realty. In real estate, Gary has developed, syndicated and invested in properties that in today's value, aggregate over $500 million.

In 1981, Gary started Capital Hill Group, Inc., a boutique investment banking firm, which is a member of FINRA and is governed by the SEC. Gary has raised over $60 million from individuals and small funds. He continues to provide investment banking services for emerging growth companies and is considered a leading expert in raising capital for both real estate and small to medium-size companies.

A native New Yorker, Gary now lives in Texas.

Contents

Part I Preparing to Make Your Fortune

Part II Nuts and Bolts

Introduction

People are always blaming their circumstances for what they are.
I don't believe in circumstances. The people who get on in the world are
people who get up and look for circumstances they want, and if they can't
find them, make them.

— George Bernard Shaw

Successful people belong to an extremely elite club. The top 1% are the winners, the ones who call the shots. They make the most money and live where and how they wish. Everyone wants to do business with the most successful individuals, and so they usually attract better opportunities than those on lower rungs.

Success for that top 1% isn't reached by accident, though. Successful people work hard to reach the top and stay there. Their success is the result of a number of other factors too, including mastery of their field, using the right systems, and staying on plan. In direct selling, these ingredients are especially important. Once you find the right company, know your products well, and stay with a selling technique that works for you, you'll find all that hard work really pays off.

In this book, I'm going to teach you a system which is common to most successful people, in direct selling and beyond. The system is made up of seven steps. Although everyone defines success differently, the steps that all successful people take tend to be alike.

The most successful people didn't get to the top by acting haphazardly. They succeeded because they anticipated, worked hard and planned. They understood that change is inevitable and that it can destroy even the best thought-out plans. Since they don't know exactly what changes will occur, they factor different scenarios into their plans and build *dynamic models for success* that enable them to quickly respond when changes come. That's what Jimmy Smith did. Jimmy is one of the most successful network marketers of all time.

A Meeting Made in Heaven

I can't wait to tell you the story about Jimmy Smith. His success in network marketing will just blow you away.

If you follow Jimmy, you'll be light-years ahead of almost everyone in direct selling. Just think: How many times does someone give you a step-by-step plan of how they made a fortune and what keeps them making tons of money every second of the day? Don't put this book down. You're going to learn the nuts and bolts of building a business from the person that's made millions of dollars doing it.

I came across Jimmy as I was starting up my latest business. Right away I could tell he was on to something big—because I've made a few million myself. I always have an eye out for the latest opportunity, and Jimmy Smith is as good as it gets.

Let me tell you a little bit about myself for a second. As crazy as it might sound, I never wanted to be in business. I originally had a bent for writing and poetry. But with a new family on the way, I soon found myself in the business trenches. Very quickly, I discovered, by working at a prestigious investment banking firm, that there were repeating patterns in business that worked. Initially, I learned these secret patterns from the senior partner, who was one of the wealthiest men of his time. He advised the Kennedys, Lyndon B. Johnson, and William Paley of CBS. The writer in me saw that certain business models—similar to scripts, characters and plots—almost always led to success. After working for this firm for a year, I got the entrepreneurial urge. I decided to test the successful business models that I had learned from my mentor.

I didn't exactly get rich right away. After two difficult partnerships in the first two years of my business career, where I made my partners millions and saw my share go into their pockets, I set out to use the successful business models for myself. I borrowed $15,000 and put myself in business. By age 31, I made enough money to semi-retire to Boca Raton, Florida, to write a novel. Yet that was only the beginning of a life-long study of patterns of success in business and in life.

This is the first of a series of Quick Steps To books where I examine a business model such as direct selling [network marketing or multi-level marketing (MLM)] and show my readers how to use it to gain great wealth. Direct selling is defined as: "a retail channel for the distribution of goods and services. At a basic level it may be defined as marketing and selling products, direct to consumers away from a fixed retail location. Sales are typically made through party plan, one to one demonstrations, and other personal contact arrangements...Direct selling is distinct from direct marketing because it is about individual sales agents reaching and dealing directly with clients." (source: Wikipedia)

In *Quick Steps To Direct Selling Success*, I feature the system of a top network marketer who has achieved the pinnacle of success—Jimmy Smith. To make sure you get the best insights, strategies, and solutions, I have also researched numerous writings on direct selling and spoken with many prominent people in the field. In this way, you will learn what makes for success in direct selling and in business in general. The terms *direct selling, network marketing* and *MLM* will be used interchangeably throughout this book.

Over the years, I've analyzed a wide variety of businesses and developed an understanding of how they work. Achieving success in business can be complex and perplexing. The secret is to break your business down into steps that can be easily understood. Then execute those steps impeccably and move on. The next time you repeat the pattern with even greater success. After all, if a former butcher could become a millionaire, so can you.

From Meats to Millions

Jimmy Smith worked for 40 years at Acme supermarkets in the Philadelphia area. Jimmy was a terrific butcher and built a beautiful family. But when he injured his back and could no longer perform the hard daily physical labor of a butcher, he was devastated. Was his life over? Jimmy wasn't willing to settle for that. He had always wanted more out of life, and so instead of resigning himself to sitting around for the rest of his life and collecting his pension, Jimmy dared to dream huge and decided to pursue another career. Only this time, he decided, he was going to be a millionaire.

He tried his hand at a few different network marketing companies. With each attempt, Jimmy got closer and closer to his dream. You see, Jimmy was not an overnight success in business. Then, at the age of 74, Jimmy joined a network marketing company called Isagenix® and proceeded to become a multimillionaire.

Jimmy's story amazed me; it was like nothing else that I had heard. So I made it a point to talk with him. We talked for hours, and what I learned about direct selling amazed me even more. Jimmy showed me the numbers and the possibilities. You could multiply your efforts into a fortune by working with other people. Since Jimmy was so successful, I said, "Jimmy, I'm going to pick your brain." Jimmy replied, "That's what it's all about. One leads and educates another."

Jimmy reminded me of my favorite grandfather, and after we spoke the first few times, I asked Jimmy if I could interview him so I wouldn't miss out on any of his wisdom. For hours he graciously told me about what he had learned. Jimmy the network-marketing master became my guru.

This book is centered around Jimmy's wisdom and knowledge. It's intended to show you that direct selling can work for you whether you are just starting out or are already a network marketer and want to reach the next level faster. Its purpose is to get you started on the road to financial success.

How to Use This Book

I've divided this book in two parts: the first is *Preparing to Make Your Fortune* and the second is *Nuts and Bolts*. The first part introduces you to Jimmy Smith and direct selling. It also gives you basic business principles that will help you succeed in the direct selling. Because, make no mistake, direct selling is a business—not just sales and distribution. One of the biggest mistakes I observed in why people fail in direct selling is that they do not truly understand business to begin with. Part II. *Nuts and Bolts* outlines specific steps that you should take in the direct selling business to accelerate your success.

As you read this book, think of how each point relates to <u>what you're trying to accomplish</u>. As you do, you'll be customizing the information in this book for your specific needs. On each subject, think about your business, its problems and ways to solve them.

If you're not yet involved in business, create a fictional business in your mind. Name it, structure it and tell yourself how it works. Visualize it; see it clearly in your mind. Then apply this book's lessons to your fictional business. You'll be surprised how visualizing will help you when you get into business for yourself.

In this book, you'll learn about *dynamic models* for success. You'll find out how to respond to any market or circumstance. I'll explain the approach that winners—the top 1% —have in common. You will master the art of anticipation: the ability to recognize patterns and clues and make the most of them in the future. You'll also discover how to forge forward when others are shrinking with fear.

So enjoy this book, and please feel free to contact me at gary.spirer@stepsto.com

Gary Spirer
Austin, TX
www.StepsTo.com

PART I

PREPARING TO MAKE YOUR FORTUNE

1

Meet Jimmy Smith

As I was working on an ebook for my website, Hank Winchester, my associate at **StepsTo.com**, called me. Hank is a savvy businessman who made a great deal of money in direct selling. He said he had just learned about an exciting opportunity with a network marketing company, Isagenix®. When he told me that it had revenues of $250 million in 2009 and that he thought it had the potential to be a billion-dollar company—suddenly, I was all ears. Hank then added, "Don't just take my word for it. Speak to Jimmy."

"Who's Jimmy?"

"Jimmy Smith was a butcher. He worked for Acme Supermarkets for 40 years before he got involved with Isagenix®. He started with Isagenix® when he was 74 years old, and now he's 82. The guy has 400,000 distributors and he's adding more every day—something like 400 plus. He and his daughters make $15,000 a day. In the past five years, he's made over $20 million."

Faster than you could say Isagenix®, I got Jimmy's phone number. He told me his story, which is weaved throughout this book to give you the steps to succeed in direct selling. So, wherever you see the caption "Jimmy says", read very carefully.

Jimmy Says:

I had been a butcher for 40 years, and at the age of 56 I hurt my back. I was laid up in the hospital for 14 days. I had degenerative disk disease, which means the cartilage between my facet joints in my back were worn out. My bone was rubbing on bone, so it was causing a lot of pain. The doctor told me if I continued to do that job, I would end up in a wheelchair. The company where I had worked for 40 years gave me my pension, plus my social security benefits. That tells you how bad my back was. They told me, "Jimmy you have served us well, you have done a good job. Go find a new career."

That was great, but at age 56 with only a high school education, I didn't find much out there. My wife suggested maybe I get a job as a crossing guard, but I didn't like that idea. I said, "No I don't think so. I think I can do better than that."

The truth was, I was devastated that I couldn't do the job that I had done my whole life. My father had done it up until he was 70, and I figured I would do it until I was at least 70. I loved that business, I loved that job. I thought that was really all I could do. I am dreamer, though. I have been a dreamer all my life. I had to make a decision, though. After 40 years of work, my pension was $2,000 a month for the rest of my life.

So I was either going to shrink my lifestyle to live on my pension or increase my income to meet my dreams. I chose the latter. I started to look at all the possibilities.

Of course, anything I wanted to do would have to be sedentary. I couldn't do any physical work. Finally, I had to start working with my brain instead of my body. I had earned my living with my body lifting meat, cutting meat and all that physical stuff.

Now I had to start using my brain to make a living. If I could find the opportunity, I told myself I could become a millionaire. That's what my dream was: someday I would become a millionaire.

When I grew up, my father was a butcher with seven kids. I grew up in a middle-class family. We had the necessities of life but nothing extra. I got married and I had six children, and then I was in the same boat. There was never anything extra.

I had always dreamed that someday I would do better. If I found something that I could really get excited about, I could become a millionaire.

Six years later, at the age of 62, a dear friend called me up and said, "Jimmy I want to take you to an opportunity meeting." I had no idea what it was all about, not a clue, but I agreed to go with him. The meeting was a multi-level marketing meeting, and the products that they were selling were water filters. The guys were real sharp. They laid out the numbers, they laid out the opportunity, and it seemed so good.

After the meeting I went up to the guy running the meeting and I said, "Is this a good deal, is this really a great opportunity?" He said, "This is the best opportunity in the world!"

I didn't buy his pitch, though. I knew enough about multi-level marketing to know that the first people you contacted were part of your family. Where's your mother? I asked. Where's your father, where's your sisters or brothers, where's your kids? Are they here? He admitted that none of them had come. So I got a little suspicious, and I declined the opportunity.

A little later another guy gave me a video called the *Don Failla Napkin Presentation*. Don Failla to this day goes all around the world teaching people geometric progression of numbers. That video was an hour and 45 minutes long, and I played it over and over and over again. Something happened to me. The mathematics of network marketing jumped out at me. Just from that one meeting and talking to this guy and watching this marketing video, I said, "Wow, network marketing is cool; this could be democracy in its finest form if it was done correctly." I made up my mind right then and there that I was going to learn everything I could about network marketing. I found out there were a lot of companies to choose from.

I started on a mission to teach myself the ropes. I wanted to be as good as I could get at network marketing, just like I wanted to be the best on the butcher block.

So I went on a mission. I joined companies, used their products and learned their compensation plans. All along the way I was teaching myself.

I read every book I could get my hands on. I watched every video, and I was determined that I was going to be successful in network marketing.

I was going to find a company that really did it correctly and then be successful and hopefully teach my six children how to do network marketing and subsequently my grandchildren. That was my mission and I am still on it. It's working out, it's really working out.

I worked 40 years as a butcher and in those years I made about $400,000. I have to work 200 years as a butcher to earn what I earned last year in Isagenix®. I would have to work 2,000 years as a butcher to earn what my family has earned in the past seven years, which is $20 million dollars. I would have to have a $100 million invested to try and get 5%. Try and get 5% today recurring residual revenues to make today, which is $5 million a year. That's royalty; I paid more income tax last year than the President earned—$405,000. That might be a clue that I finally found the right business.

Speaking with Jimmy changed my life. It whet my appetite to learn all about direct selling. So like Jimmy, I went on a mission. I studied direct selling in great detail and found that it could do wonders. Through direct selling, people could make millions, and in this book I'll tell you how.

2

Business 101

"Your chances of success in any undertaking can always be measured by your belief in yourself."

—Robert Collier

Success has two essential ingredients. It takes (1) talented, determined people who (2) follow a system and/or plan. The most savvy business operators know the current climate, understand the rules and have a plan.

We are now in an interesting business climate. I call it the "Performance Economy." Today, people are obsessed with celebrities and everyone wants to be a star. Star power creates financial power—big stars bring in big bucks. Just look at *American Idol, Dancing with the Stars, America's Got Talent,* all the cooking and reality television shows and endless designer labels. Star-based goods and services dominate the markets and make gazillions of dollars.

The Performance Economy is based on a simple formula that has filtered down from the top. Business operators on every level—huge to tiny, local to global—want to be stars. They want to become celebrities, build name recognition, and they essentially follow the same plan. When you understand that formula, it will help you reach the top.

Let's examine *American Idol* and its format. I'm sure you know how the show goes—almost everyone on the planet does—but let me describe it in business terms.

American Idol is a contest to find the next singing superstar. Contestants enter to land a recording contract and launch singing careers. Hopefuls line up by the tens of thousands to audition in selected major cities and appear on the show. Those who make the cut go to Hollywood, where the roster is further whittled down. After a few weeks, the show finally gets rolling and the public votes on which singers will be eliminated. Each ensuing week, one candidate is eliminated and the last one left standing wins. He or she is the American Idol.

Great formula. Remarkably popular and successful show! So how can you use its success to help you in direct selling?

Forging Links

American Idol uses a formula that I call *core magnets*. This is the product or service that attracts you—customer, investor—to a business. They are the stars of the show, the reason you come to watch or to buy or sign up from someone else. Without core magnets like an iPod or iPhone, where would Apple be? Where would Google be without its search algorithm and its AdWords system?

Core magnets are the key to *all* successful businesses, the vital links that all businesses need to succeed. Core magnets have targets—objects that they attract. *American Idol*'s "target" is the audience, the people out in TV land. Like all TV shows, *American Idol* wants to attract the largest possible audience.

The target for businesses is customers. Without customers, businesses fail. To reach their targets, businesses need core magnets. In direct selling especially, one of the most important core magnets often overlooked is YOU. Because direct selling is largely a people business, you are a key factor in whether you will attract or repel customers.

Just as *American Idol* contestants must stand out, so must you. Not only must they shine, but they must continually convince their targets, the voting audience, that they deserve their support. Week after week, they must demonstrate that they have the star power make it to the top.

To win in most businesses, especially direct selling, you need to use your talents, knowledge and skills in a similar way. Do you have a unique personality and style? Are you willing to take a risk and get on stage? You will see that there are similar characteristics in Jimmy and other star successes in business.

Let's use the *American Idol* analogy to see how you can attract people. To become the next *American Idol*, a contestant must display a combination of his or her talent, style, looks, personality and likeability. The winner must:

1. *Be able to sing*. Singing is each contestant's product, his or her stock in trade. The reason the singers sing is to entertain. To win, a singer must entertain and be as good or better than the competition. The *American Idol* audience wants to be entertained and those who can't sing a lick won't win.

    Now let's look at products. The products you are selling must provide what customers want—Tupperware must withstand being used over and over again, and food must be nutritious and taste good. Quality counts! If you are not sure that the products you are selling are top-notch, you picked the wrong company.

2. *Have a unique style*. A contestant must be distinctive to emerge from the pack. If everyone operates similarly, no one will stand out. Likewise, if customers can get the same result from everyone, they won't have any reason to buy from you. You won't be able to build loyalty and long-term relationships. Don't try to sell something that you can buy at Target.

3. *Choose the right songs*. They say "timing is everything" and it frequently is. Most people don't want to buy winter coats in the summer; they don't even want to try them on. Entertainers must offer what audiences want, they type of music they want to hear. The most brilliant young classical cellist would be voted off *American Idol*. Similarly, a business must provide what their customers want and need. If you're trying to sell a water filter that is so complex to

install that your customers need to call a plumber, how many water filters do you think people will buy?

4. *Connect with the audience*. In a world of choices, we tend to gravitate to a select few. Often, we can't articulate why we're drawn to them, but we just seem to connect. Certain people stand out and are more memorable; they make a stronger impression on you. That same principle can be carried over to direct selling in a practical fashion. Market research is essential. Identify your audience and learn what they want. Find out your competitive advantages and build your sales around them.

5. *Have star quality.* People want the best and will often pay a premium for the best. Look at the luxury market and the unbelievable prices people will pay. Become the star of your level, the best in class or group. Make your products or services better, provide more value for the price, have great customer service, few returns and the most pleasant employees. Find ways to stand out.

QUICK STEPS: *YOU MUST HAVE A HOOK OR MAGNET TO ATTRACT AND KEEP CUSTOMERS.*

In business, customers vote with their time, money and resources. Simply put, for businesses to succeed they must attract (magnetize) their targets (their customers) and once they hook them, they must retain them.

Let's go back to what Jimmy said.

You will see how the fundamentals of business and the same traits of winning contestants on *American Idol* are the same that Jimmy follows:

1. Find an opportunity: Jimmy believed that he had to find the right opportunity—not any opportunity

2. Believe you can succeed: Most success can be traced to the inner belief you can succeed even before you start, or somewhere in the process you get an inspiration. Jimmy said he wanted to become a

millionaire, and as he learned more about network marketing, he started to believe he could succeed.

3. Be open to opportunity and seize it when it comes: Once Jimmy heard Don Failla's presentation on network marketing and its potential, he went for it.

4. Be passionate about what you choose to do: Jimmy looked for an opportunity about which he could become passionate.

5. Dare To Dream Huge: Jimmy had a dream to be more. To become a millionaire with no prospects for work was a huge dream.

Jimmy Says: "Watch out for dream stealers! Dream stealers like you the way you are—broke and busy. They fear change, so they do not want to see you build this business, either out of jealousy, over-protection or both. Don't tell them your plans. Just sell them your products."

QUICK STEPS: *THE PSYCHOLOGY NEEDED TO SUCCEED IN DIRECT SELLING.*

Think in terms of the long run, not just today. Focus on building an enduring business, not just on making a quick score. Watch out for get-rich-quick schemes. Usually, they don't work and they often set you back. Instead, know what you want. Set goals, conduct research and plan. Be patient, but persistent. If one approach doesn't work, be flexible and try something else. Build slowly, solidly and for the long run.

Have a purpose. Know what you want and why you want it. Know specifically and don't be vague. Then go after it.

Be passionate about your business. Let your emotions inspire and motivate you. When you are passionate, other people will notice. They will listen to you, join you and spread the word. Passion and enthusiasm are contagious.

Be open to criticism. Solicit the opinions of your customers, distributors and others on how well your business is serving them. Let them be the judges and listen to them. Find out what they want, need and how you can provide it better.

Expect rejection, but don't let it stop you. Obstacles, setbacks and mistakes are a part of business and life. Learn from them. The trick is not to let them defeat you. When you get "no" for an answer, find out what it takes to get a "yes." Fix the problem or mistake and then focus your efforts in continually getting "yeses."

Always keep learning and studying your craft. To excel in business, to rise to the very top, you must become an expert and know everything possible about your field. You must become the leading expert so you can solve all the problems, learn all the shortcuts and see what tomorrow will bring.

Dare to dream huge. Don't settle or just get by. Be ambitious and shoot for the stars. Leave your mark and do something important that will change lives. Be an important person who will make a major difference. Don't hold back.

3

The Seven Steps to Wealth

Let me tell you a secret. A time-tested formula exists for getting rich is *build assets and then income.* Most people try to do it backwards and never hit it big. I learned this secret from Andre Meyer, a mentor of mine who was one of the wealthiest men in the world.

First, find your Golden Goose. It's the asset that will create your income or your Golden Eggs.

What does that mean? In the fable, a farmer owned the Golden Goose and he was impatient to get the Golden Eggs faster. He decided to kill the Golden Goose and open it up. That's what happens with many businesses that are created. They are focused on the Golden Eggs, but they forget there has to be the Golden Goose—what supports the production of the products or services, or the Golden Eggs.

People are impatient. They want to get rich quick and don't want to spend the time and resources to build assets, or what will earn you money. Building assets takes time, but unless you inherit a fortune, building assets is the only way to acquire great wealth. So build your Golden Goose first because when you do, it will keep cranking out those Golden Eggs and you'll have a direct pipeline to the bank.

If you have a Golden Goose, it will make money. And the money it makes, each Golden Egg, will also make money. You'll have a money-making machine. Over time, your income, the Golden Eggs, will compound and that's how you'll get really rich.

In direct selling, that means you must choose your company wisely. Pick products that will sell often so that you can reorder often. Luckily, your ability to produce Golden Eggs can be multiplied by all the people you sign up under you, or your downline. You may not get as many people in your downline as Jimmy Smith, but remember, each one of those people wants to sign up people under their downline. So your profits can grow exponentially—if you choose the right Golden Goose.

QUICK STEPS: *BUILD ASSETS FIRST.*

Wealth is all about building and owning assets. Assets by definition produce income whether you work for them or not. The business you enter, as well as all investments you make, must work for you.

Most people never build wealth because they try to build on the money they earn from their jobs. They can't get rich solely through their wages because the money they earn is not enough to leverage, or multiply. Leveraging occurs when you reach lots of people (for example, the target audience you attract with your core magnets—your great products or services which your customers can't do without) with a minimum of effort and expense.

Leverage usually means you borrow money, such as when you finance your home or car with a loan, but it can also mean that you use resources other than your own such as other people's talents, knowledge, skills or resources—the beauty of direct selling is that it allows you to do just that!

People can't leverage themselves or their hours because they're only building from one source, themselves, and their allotted time. Usually, all or most of their income goes to just keeping them afloat. This is where Jimmy had found himself after 40 years working as a butcher—he only had so many hours in a day to work; he could not leverage himself.

I'll get into leverage more in Chapter 7, but leverage is the key to business success and wealth. It's really exciting. It's what direct selling is all about. If you want to know about leverage and can't wait, go get my free special report called "Mastering the Art of Leverage." Here's the link: **http://www.masteringtheartofleverage.com/** or **www.StepsTo.com**

So, if you can't become wealthy by trading your hours for money, then you have to get wealthy another way. That's where the Golden Goose, the asset, comes in. The Golden Goose becomes the vehicle to a successful business and wealth. The Golden Goose is what you leverage and grow. It's not you alone, which is the major reason why so few people are wealthy.

To eliminate costly trial and error that can take years, I have created a system that all top entrepreneurs, business operators and investors follow to build their vehicles to wealth.

The 7 Steps to Wealth System

To build your asset, follow these seven steps:

Step 1. *Idea*

It all starts with the idea. Ideas are the seeds from which great businesses and fortunes bloom. Howard Schultz dotted the world with Starbucks as Ray Kroc did with McDonald's. Ruth Handler dreamed up the Barbie doll and Southwest Airlines gave us low-cost, bare-bones airfares. They all hit it huge and their creations became household names.

Ideas can come from many sources, and in many sizes and shapes. They can develop over time or come to you in a flash. Your idea doesn't have to be for a totally new invention, you don't have to reinvent the wheel or the iPad. You could look for a company that has simply refined something, making it better, easier, smaller, lighter or cheaper. In fact, most great ideas are small changes or unique twists on existing products or services. Google did not have the first search engine, nor did they invent the AdWords concept. What Google did was to get it right first.

That's the key—whoever gets it right first, wins.

When you survey direct selling companies, they all started from simple ideas. Much of what they market is similar, but the successful ones have the unique twist—a better formulation—that becomes their winning solution (core magnet) to a problem others have, such as Isagenix® and weight loss.

Step 2. *Design*

After you come up with an idea, you need to be able to describe it to others so that they understand exactly what it is. You want to choose the best, most customer-friendly design, one with strong customer appeal. If you want to sell a new drink, the next Red Bull, look for a recipe that customers will love. Look for vivid sketches of your clothing line or easy-to-follow specifications for a home recycling system that will excite others.

Without a design, an idea isn't real—it is only in your head. No one can manufacture or provide it. If you can't describe your idea, you won't be able to interest others in it. So they won't buy it, or tell others about it. The right design forces a company to examine its product in great detail, find its flaws and problems and refine them.

Look at winning products in direct selling. Take Isagenix®, the company that Jimmy markets. Their products are well designed .They have a clean health-oriented appearance that complements their superior health products. Their products themselves are designed with superior formulations. The same with their marketing materials.

You find superior design in direct selling and direct selling companies such as Avon, Xango, Mary Kay and MonaVie.

Yet, design extends beyond products and services. Design is how you plan your business—your strategies, techniques and tactics. The best direct selling companies have well-designed compensation plans.

Step 3. _Discovery_

This is the exploration and testing stage when you gather information to support your idea and design. Will it fly? It's where you look for flaws and how to best fix them. During discovery you also identify your market, your competitors and your competitive advantages. Will people buy it and for how much?

The business term for discovery is "doing due diligence." It means examining your venture meticulously and from every angle. At this point, learn everything possible about your item and uncover all problems because later on, you may not be able to answer questions people have or have to refund their money. Thoroughness is the key in the discovery stage.

In direct selling, you have to know what the strengths and weaknesses of your competition are. If you don't know, your potential customers may. They can go on the Internet and find out in a minute. If you are looking to choose a direct selling company or move to a new one, you need to do your homework—and only settle for the best.

Step 4. _Development_

In development a business creates a prototype for its goods and services, which will bring them to life. The prototype gives an idea substance and makes it concrete. If you are trying to sell a new product in a company's line, it gives you something tangible to show others, gauge their interest and get their feedback. Their reaction can make or break the new product.

The developmental phase is the most critical stage in the process. A good company makes sure to invest sufficient time, effort and resources to do it right. Many businesses fail because they rush this stage, skimp or don't do it well enough.

In looking at direct selling companies, a large percentage of them fail very quickly. A big selling point of many new direct selling companies is that they are offering a ground-floor opportunity for those new to direct selling as well as those who are seasoned veterans. But most of the time, you never get a roof over your head because the ground-floor opportunity never materializes. This is true of most new business ventures—not just direct selling.

The same goes for you. You really begin to understand direct selling once you get involved. When the bloom is off the rose, you begin to see you are in a competitive business where there is no quick, easy money.

Step 5. *Pre-launch*

In this phase, you approach your audience, get their attention and capture their interest. Get them to feel that they are the first to see your item, that they are in on the ground floor. Build buzz. Consider this the start of your promotional campaign and your last chance to test the public reaction before your products or services hit the street.

Expect problems during the pre-launch stage. Few introductions go as planned. Anticipate all that could go wrong and have fixes to your pitch that you can quickly implement. When problems crop up, view them as opportunities, chances to fine-tune your pitches so that they will be huge hits.

This is the best of times and the worst of times. You jump into the market with the new product and start testing your wings. You begin to tell others more and more about your new direct selling company and opportunity.

Wow! You didn't immediately get them lining up to buy what you got. In fact, to some, you are selling the plague. To others, you are a savior. Whatever the responses, you see that certain words and scripts work better than others. Jimmy will come to the rescue as we get into more and more of what makes for success in direct selling.

Step 6. *Launch*

Congratulations, your company's goods and service have been rolled out and are now available to customers. You've ironed out the kinks in your approach and are now making your big sales push. Expect some hurdles.

Few launches are completely problem-free. Find out how to get over the hurdles and learn from them.

The timing of a launch is critical, so plan it carefully. Study your market, estimate the demand and discover your competitors' plans. Strategize. Figure out the best time and places to launch and how big it should be. Try not to introduce your company's new summer wear in the middle of winter or when the competition is releasing their latest lines.

You are now selling your products and services. Sometimes you get immediate sales. Sometimes you get none. This is the easiest time to get discouraged and feel like nothing is going right. In the launch, everything might seem much more difficult than you thought. Again, in direct selling this is to be expected. Sales take time in any new business, or can be sometimes slow in existing businesses. If you don't keep your eyes open, you won't get sales consistently.

Step 7. _Post-launch_

Finally, your products or services are selling and revenues are rolling in, but your work is far from done. Assess the market's reaction to your items. Why did people buy or not buy? What do buyers like and dislike? What would they prefer? What follow-up products would they buy?

Now that you have consumers' attention, engage them. Learn how you can improve.

Survey customers; speak with them one-to-one. Find out what adjustments and improvements are needed, which would be easy and which would require major overhauls. Use the post-launch period to build a strong base of loyal, repeat customers.

Most businesses are terrible when it comes to follow-up. This means follow-up as to leads and customers alike. In direct selling it is imperative to follow up constantly and keep your potential and existing customers engaged.

What I want you to take away from the 7 Steps to Wealth System is that they apply to any business or opportunity that you want to evaluate, start up, grow or attract investors to. If you apply them in the sequence I laid out, you'll find that these 7 steps work to allow you to build your own Golden Goose. Go get my *Speed to Your Wealth Course* to learn more about how the 7 Steps to Wealth System can help you evaluate any opportunity. Here is the link: **www.7stepstowealth.com.**

4

Attitude, Motivation and Goals

Are you familiar with the 1% rule? It says that only one of 100 people will become rich (1%). Just 5%—5 out of 100 people—will become financially independent. So, when you get involved in any business at any stage—but especially during the beginning stage—the odds are heavily weighed against you.

Before you can become a direct selling success, you have to set your goals. You want to be in that 1% bracket? Then do what successful people have been doing for years: set up targets so you'll know where you're going.

Jimmy Smith studied over and over Earl Nightingale's classic 1956 book, *The Strangest Secret.* Nightingale wrote:

> We live in a golden age. This is an era that humanity has looked forward to, dreamed of, and worked toward for thousands of years. We live in the richest era that ever existed on the face of the earth…
>
> However, if you take 100 individuals who start even at the age of 25, do you have any idea what will happen to those men and women by the time they are 65?

These people believe they're going to be successful. They are eager toward life, there is a certain sparkle in their eye, an erectness in their courage, and life seems like a pretty interesting adventure to them.

But by the time they're 65, only one will be rich, four will be financially independent, five will still be working and 54 will be broke—depending on others for life necessities.

Although times and the economic climate have changed, the numbers still hold today—only 1% are truly wealthy. Nightingale wrote, "The difference is *goals*. People with goals succeed because they know where they're going. It's that simple. Failures believe that their lives are shaped by circumstances ... by things that happen to them ... by exterior forces."

Write Down Your Goals

A study conducted by Gail Matthews at Dominican University called "Written Goal Study" confirmed that those who put their goals in writing accomplished significantly more than those who did not. Jimmy Smith learned about goal setting from reading Napoleon Hill and Earl Nightingale, his two favorite authors.

You recall that Jimmy told me his first goal was to learn the ropes if he was going to become a millionaire in network marketing. He set the goal of constantly educating himself. He read what the best had to say and what they did.

Jimmy had a definite purpose or aim. Napoleon Hill in his classic book *Think and Grow Rich* says that is where success in business and finance starts.

Success starts in your mind. Jimmy said that he could no longer do physical labor. He had to turn to his mind and train it to keep focused on the goals he set. Since Jimmy knew where he was going, he could use all his energies to get where he wanted to go.

QUICK STEPS: *HAVE SPECIFIC GOALS.*

Write down specific goals. Clearly identify your target and keep your eyes on it. It makes a difference. At the firing range, you don't look all around. You focus on the target. You lift your rifle, put it in position and take a deep breath. Then you slowly squeeze the trigger. All the while, you steadily eye the center of the bull's-eye—otherwise you miss.

Writing your goals clarifies them and gives you something specific to shoot for. It helps you be accountable and to commit to reaching your goals. Some people announce their goals to their friends, they tell them to the world, because it motivates them to focus and concentrate on toward reaching them. Go get my *Speed to Your Wealth Action Plan* to get the exact steps needed to reach your goals. Here is the link: **www.7stepstowealthsystem.com.**

Motivation

To succeed in business, something must motivate and drive you. A flame must burn within you; it must fire your engine and propel you on. Your motivation may be money—most people's is. It may be the fact that you find a compelling interest, something that captivates and takes hold of you. To reach the very top, some force within you must exist that pushes you to succeed.

The process is the same in business as it is in mountain climbing. You must be prepared to work and really want it to climb all the way to the top. Most people won't make the effort. They don't care enough to scale the peak. To get to the top, you must be motivated; you must passionately want it.

> **QUICK STEPS:** *BE PASSIONATE ABOUT YOUR CUSTOMER AND MAKING MONEY.*
>
> Be both solution-oriented for your customers and money–oriented for your business.
>
> Customers are motivated by solutions. Business is about making money. If you have other goals, then your venture is more like a hobby than a business. If you go into business, you must make money by providing superior solutions or you won't stay in business long.

When you're highly motivated, your efforts don't seem like work. You're doing what you want and must do. Usually, you don't question or doubt the time you put in; you just forge ahead. When you encounter roadblocks, you find ways to overcome them.

In order to succeed, all that you do, every step you take, must be aligned with your purpose. It must be pointed toward your goal.

Jimmy Smith was motivated by physical pain. He was 56, at an age when many people are planning their retirement. His body could no longer take the pounding that a butcher absorbs. Jimmy didn't want to throw in the towel, stop working, retire and radically change his life. He had always lived a physically active life. Inactivity depressed him.

So Jimmy decided to look forward rather than look back. He decided to envision a new world and a new life. Instead of looking back, making excuses and wallowing in self-pity, as he easily could have, Jimmy looked forward and followed a positive model—his father.

"My father worked into his 70s, so I knew that I could work until I was at least 70." Jimmy knew that he had time and was convinced that he could succeed. At 82, he's still going strong—and getting richer than King Midas.

Strong Belief

The most successful people, the top 1%, share a common characteristic: they strongly believe that they will succeed. The key word is "*strongly*." They don't just believe, they have a powerful, overriding belief. They are absolutely certain that regardless of the obstacles, they will succeed. Those who are the most successful set goals, envision their success, and no matter what happens, regardless of the hurdles, they plow on toward success.

When Jimmy left Acme, he examined his options and what he could do. When he inventoried his assets, he realized that his most important asset was his mind. He wanted to put his mind to use. He didn't want to retire, go out to pasture or merely scrape by. Jimmy still wanted to be in the game. More than that, he wanted to be a major player. He has a good story on this subject, so I'll let him tell it in his own words:

I had a good friend whose name was Jay McDowell. He had played football for the Philadelphia Eagles in 1948 and 1949, the first and only time they ever won back-to-back championships...He was quite an athlete, a real big, strong, tough guy, but he was very shy.

After football, he had to make a living, so he chose insurance. In order for him to get over his shyness, the company gave him two records. One was based on the book *Think and Grow Rich* by Napoleon Hill, and the other was *The Strangest Secret* by Earl Nightingale. He told me about them at my first network marketing meeting. He was the celebrity guest at that meeting. He said, "Jimmy, I became a very good insurance salesman because I listened to them over and over again. I think they'll help you."

I had been a butcher my whole life, and my biggest fear at that time was getting up in front of people and talking. I didn't think I'd ever be able to do it.

I listened to those two records almost every night before I went to bed. Bridget [Jimmy's wife] really thought I was cracking up. She'd see these records and call up the kids. "I think your father lost it. He's possessed with getting rich."

I wasn't so much possessed with getting rich. I was trying to get out of a box, this box I'd been in for 40 years. I thought the only thing I could ever do to make a living was cut meat. I'll tell you, these are the two most powerful CDs I've ever heard in my entire life.

Think and Grow Rich is the number one motivational book ever written. It's been a bestseller for years and years and years. It has influenced some of the most successful people in the history of our country.

Another influence on me came about because of an odd coincidence. I went to King of Prussia, north of Philadelphia, to see Zig Ziglar and Brian Tracy speak. When Zig Ziglar walked out on stage, he said, "I used to be a butcher." I almost jumped out of my seat. Then he said, "I worked my way up to meat manager." I thought, "Wow, I worked my way up to meat supervisor. I was better than you."

After listening to him speak for four hours, I made up my mind. "Someday I'm going to stand up on a stage and do just what he's doing. If that old butcher can do it, this young butcher can do it."

Then I listened to Brian Tracy for four hours, and he was unbelievable too. I was on a pension, so I didn't have a lot of money, but I had a credit card. On the way out, I bought $350 worth of cassettes and videotapes. I had to sneak them into the house so my wife didn't see them. I couldn't tell her I paid $90 to go hear two guys speak. She would have me committed.

Yet it turned out to be one of the best things I've ever done because I've never been the same since. I started watching Brian Tracy's videos at night down in my finished basement. I'd be down there by myself watching videos. I was on a mission; I really was. Once people understand network marketing as clearly as I do, I don't know how they could ever do anything else.

> **QUICK STEPS:** *THINK RICH TO GROW RICH.*
>
> Your mind is your greatest asset. It's key to your happiness and success. Your mind works exclusively for you 24/7/365, and it can bring you ongoing income, rewards and fulfillment.

Your mind can motivate you or hold you back. It can free you or imprison you. Your mind can drive you to succeed or riddle you with fear, doubt and indecision. They say, "You are who you think you are," which means that the decision is up to you. You control your future. It's your choice whether to move forward or hang back. It's a matter of attitude and it's strictly up to you.

Harness the power of your mind, utilize your greatest asset, think positively, adjust your attitude—give it your best shot!

Asking Hard Questions

"I looked around, I looked around, I looked around," Jimmy told me. "I asked myself what I could do." Jimmy knew he had to make big changes, but he had no idea what they might be. He knew that he had to be brutally honest with himself, since he no longer could work as a butcher. He had to come up with an idea and design a new game plan. He had to ask better questions.

QUICK STEPS: *TAKE A BRUTALLY HONEST*
SELF-ASSESSMENT AND REAP THE REWARDS.

Be honest with yourself regardless how much it might hurt. Assess your personal assets realistically. Identify the areas in which you excel. Don't delude yourself or force your way into areas that you're not qualified or prepared for. Identify your assets, your talents, skills, knowledge and capabilities. Then build on them. When you taste success, you can switch gears and examine whether you want to venture off in new directions.

QUICK STEPS: *ASK OTHERS TO ASSESS YOU,*
BUT BE CAREFUL WHO YOU ASK.

Ask people who you work with to identify your strengths. Most people are poor self-evaluators; they are not realistic and are surprised at the answers they receive. Other people are more realistic and will more accurately tell you what your assets are.

Jimmy asked, "Where am I now?" He saw that he was in a box. When he asked himself where he wanted to be, he concluded that he wanted to create a better life for himself.

Jimmy recognized he would have to learn, educate himself and evaluate new opportunities.

Education comes in many forms, so decide which is best for you. Your decision will depend on your circumstances, whether you can go to school, train or apprentice, study on your own or any combination of them. How you proceed, the route you take, is not as important as the fact that you continue to learn. Feed your mind daily.

According to recent studies, natural-born talent alone usually won't get you to the top. You must hone that talent and marry it with knowledge and skills. That means you must practice, get hands-on experience and continue to learn. It's a matter of trial and error and learning from your mistakes.

Look at great achievers. Their success didn't occur overnight. It wasn't accidental—it was the product of years of hard work. Even young geniuses like Mozart, Bill Gates and Tiger Woods had to hone their talents and master their skills. They didn't start out being superstars. They constantly studied, intensively practiced and continually learned. They worked tirelessly to perfect their knowledge and skills.

QUICK STEPS: *GO FOR IT! GET FEEDBACK.*
ADJUST AND REFINE. TRY AGAIN.

Set specific goals, obtain immediate feedback adjust from what you learned and focus on perfecting your own style and technique to get to the top.

QUICK STEPS: *KEEP LEARNING THE BASICS.*
DO NOT TRY TO TAKE SHORTCUTS.

All top achievers learned the basics—their craft—before they developed their individual style. Too often, people and companies put style over substance and, as a result, fail.

MARY KAY ASH

In the early 1960s, Mary Kay Ash faced a situation all too familiar to women. After 25 years in the direct selling business, she left her position when yet another man she had trained was promoted above her at twice her salary.

Sitting at a kitchen table, Mary Kay made two lists on a yellow legal pad. One contained the good things she had seen in business and the other featured those she thought could be improved. When she reviewed the list, she realized she had created a marketing plan for a dream company.

With just $5,000 in savings, Mary Kay Ash enlisted the help of her 20-year-old son Richard and created Beauty by Mary Kay. It was a first—a company dedicated to making life more beautiful for women. It was founded on the principle of praising people to success and on placing faith first, family second and career third. It was a company, as Mary Ash would say, "with heart."

With dedication and hard work, Mary Kay nurtured her dream from a small direct sales company to one of the largest direct sellers of skin care and cosmetics in the United States. *Fortune* magazine recognized the company as one of the 100 best companies to work for in America.

Today the vision of Mary Kay continues to help women achieve their potential and bring their dreams to life. With 1.8 million independent beauty consultants in more than 30 markets worldwide, the company continues to be one of the greatest success stories in the business. (Source: Mary Kay. www.MARYKAY.com)

5
Learning = Saturation + Repetition

"I want to stay green, because when I'm green, I'm growing. When I start to ripen, I rot."

— Ray Kroc, founder of McDonald's

People succeed not to get rich quick, but because they have a burning desire to educate themselves to be the best at what they do.

Most people don't truly understand the learning process. They think all they have to do is read, see or hear something in order to get it down cold. Unfortunately, that's not how learning works, because what rushes in frequently tends to leave just as fast.

Many people lack the patience to study and learn. They want everything to come easily, instantly, with a minimum of work. However, learning, and especially learning major skills, those that can dramatically improve your life, tends to take time and effort.

Learning is about gaining understanding and making knowledge your own. Not just for a moment, a few days or even a week, but for the long-term. Learning is about building a base and then adding to it, piece-by-piece, until something substantial emerges. It's building knowledge. As you progress, you need to make sure you understand each step and how it fits into the overall picture. To retain knowledge, learn how each component works.

QUICK STEPS: *LEARN PROPERLY.*

To learn more accurately and faster, see the big picture and the small picture (the details).

Many times when you make errors, you are amazed that you never stepped back and looked at the big picture. Or, you got the big picture but never asked what are the details or the fine print that could change the picture for the worst.

Learning usually requires repetition, continuous exposure to a subject until you understand it well. Reading a manual or a book, watching a video or doing something hands-on can be a good start, but you generally have to repeat the process over and over before the message fully sinks in. In direct selling, that means you need to know your products down cold. When you are an expert, people will respect your answers to their questions.

Jimmy's Journey: Opportunity Knocks

When Jimmy started to explore business opportunities, he attended a multi-level marketing meeting. At the meeting, he spoke with people about network marketing. It was his introduction to the subject. What he learned at the meeting intrigued him and made him want to learn more about network marketing and how it worked. So he took home a video that explained it.

The video ran for an hour forty-five minutes, and Jimmy ran it over and over and over again. Day after day, night after night, Jimmy repeatedly watched the tape and he noticed a change occurring within him. He understood that if he found two people to work under him, they in turn could find two people. So now he would have six people. He would get a percentage of every product they sold. The percentage of all those products sold was pretty hefty, and every time someone found two more people to work under him . . . well, Jimmy could get rich this way. He found his mind setting down a new track and he started to think in a different way. The network marketing video introduced Jimmy to the concept of geometric leveraging, and when he realized its power, he was hooked. He knew it could lead him to the "promised land."

Geometric leverage or leveraging sounds pretty complicated, but it's really just simple math. Think of it this way. Which way would you like your money to grow: 2 to 4 to 6 to 8 to 10 to 12 OR 2 to 4 to 8 to 16 to 32 to 64? The first growth pattern is linear, where you add 2 each time—not multiply. So, I'm sure you would pick growth pattern two, which grows by multiples or what they call geometrically. Another example of geometric growth is 2 x 2 x 2 x 2 x 2 x 2 = 64. You can put this also as 2 to the 5th power, which means you multiply the number 2 by itself five times.

So Jimmy repeatedly watched and studied the tape. He wanted to understand everything it covered about network marketing. Jimmy was excited by his new way of thinking, how saturated in it he was, and he realized that it was pulling him out of the box where he had been stuck. Now, he could look at the world differently. The more Jimmy watched the video, the more it drove, motivated and compelled him to want to master network marketing.

Perseverance

Learning takes perseverance, which many people feel they don't have. Often, fear and worry blocks you from your real aim.

When we learn something new, it is often confusing and complex. Occasionally, it's just plain hard. When some folks run into any difficulties, they get discouraged, throw up their arms and walk away.

Others stick with it—they plow ahead. Doggedly, they continue riding over the bumps until the fog clears and the road becomes smooth and straight.

Mostly, it comes down to how badly you want something. You can easily think of times in your life you wanted a certain outfit or a certain guy or girl. Nothing could stop you until you got what you wanted.

That's perseverance.

Jimmy knew nothing about network marketing and leveraging, but since he had been a butcher, he was well grounded in basic math. Simple numbers didn't scare him, they excited him. "The networking marketing numbers jumped out at me. I thought, wow, network marketing is cool."

The numbers were extraordinary. They told Jimmy that he could become fabulously rich with just a small investment. After 40 years of dealing with one customer at a time, Jimmy realized that:

1. Network marketing in its finest form could really work and generate enough income to make him a millionaire.

2. But only if it was done correctly.

So Jimmy made a commitment. He vowed to learn how to do network marketing correctly. To find the winning formula, he dedicated himself to studying, learning and practicing until he got it right.

"I made up my mind right then and there that I was going to learn everything I could about network marketing," Jimmy relates. "At that point I knew nothing. I found out that there were a lot of companies to choose from. I started on a mission to teach myself the ropes. I wanted to be as good as I could get at network marketing just like I wanted to be the best butcher on the block."

Jimmy immediately began to learn, learn, and learn some more. His focus was not on getting rich quickly. He wanted to master network marketing, to do it right. "So I joined companies, I used their products, learned their compensation plans," Jimmy said. He taught himself by reading every book he could find, watching every video and speaking with other industry insiders. Jimmy was determined, he put in the work and it really paid off.

QUICK STEPS: *BECOME A MASTER.*

Dedicate yourself to learning how to do something the right way. If you want to succeed in direct selling or any business or endeavor, dare to dream huge and set your standards to be commensurate with your dream. Once you get used to wanting to be the best, you start to find remarkable success.

The Top Requirements for Success

I've laid out for you a number of fundamentals that constantly repeat to create success for the top entrepreneurs, business operators and investors. You see them in Jimmy and other top producers in direct selling or any other type of business or undertaking:

1. Having the right mindset, a positive attitude and thinking and dreaming huge

2. Being totally committed

3. Being passionate

4. Having purpose

5. Practice

6. Having vision

7. Being patient

8. Building your base

9. Constantly educating yourself

10. Setting and writing goals.

All of the above factors are important, but they will amount to little more than a good learning experience if you choose the wrong opportunity.

6
Business Today

Technology has shifted the balance in business.

Until recently businesses were on top while customers had little clout.

Businesses dictated what goods and services they would produce, set their specifications and price, and declared when and where they would be made available. Customers took what they could get.

Mass production and mass advertising was controlled by companies with large resources. It was tough for smaller companies to become large. If a company broke through the pack, it took time and a lot of capital.

Now the world has all changed.

Technology has not only changed the playing field, it's leveled it and invented an entirely new game. It's made competition fierce, cutthroat.

Now, as soon as new goods or services hit the street, competitors can produce virtually the identical items faster, cheaper and deliver them quickly nearly anywhere on earth. As a result, international powerhouses, legendary companies that were studied and revered, have been undercut by smaller, leaner competitors.

As our world has become interconnected, businesses have been forced to reinvent themselves over and over in order to survive. Product manufacturers from IBM on down have become service companies and one size no longer fits all. Businesses now customize their services to fit individual customers' needs. Salespeople are now consultants who instruct their employers how to develop products for their customers. They often work at their customers' sites and are thought of as members of their customers' families.

It's all changed. If you go out and try the same old tactics, you're going to fall flat and you may not be able to get back up.

The key to business today is being customer-centric. You have to find the BIG IDEA or solution, which I have defined as the core magnet. Here's the way you can find the core magnets:

To find a BIG IDEA or core magnet (a superior solution), ask what your customers need and then find out how to give it to them in ways that others can't match. In direct selling, one of your biggest decisions is to choose a company to represent that truly has a solution to a problem that customers will buy—not just a bunch of distributors (those that buy and resell products to other distributors as well as customers). Ask what percentage of the direct selling company's sales are directly to customers and not to other distributors. A direct selling company that has a real solution that customers are paying money for will have more customers than they do distributors—a key indicator of whether you have a real product or just a promotion with little true value.

Jimmy says:

Picking the right company was a long process. I had to learn about what's a good product and what's a bad product. I realized that a water filter sits on your counter for three years. That's not a good product to sell with network marketing. I don't know how somebody started a company and spent millions of dollars for a water filter that lasts for three years. I mean, where's the recurring residual revenues? You have to have a product that people use on a daily basis. You have to have a product that people will buy whether they do the business or not.

Next, I realized that in network marketing you have to have a product that has an emotional impact. Weight loss is visual, and I figured if it's emotional and visual, that's a double-whammy.

Seven and a half years ago, I realized the number one health problem in the world today is overweight and obesity. A billion people worldwide are seriously overweight, and over thirty percent of them are obesely overweight. In the United States, 200 million out of 300 million people are overweight, and 34 percent of them are obesely overweight.

When I found Isagenix®, I realized how important it was...I know that everybody, if they just use the product, will benefit from it just like I did.

Getting Attention

According to the late business guru Peter Drucker, all business comes down to innovation and marketing. We have addressed some of the important issues related to innovation when I've discussed the importance of your idea/solution/core magnet.

But without the marketing/distribution, how will your customers know you exist or have a way to get your product?

Today, the biggest challenge is how to get and keep customers' attention.

Let's look at one of the main keys to business distribution. Distribution is getting both your message and your products or services out.

To succeed in business, consumers have to hear about your items before they buy. Essentially, you start with a two-step process:

- First, you reach them. You get their attention to let them know that your goods exist.

- Second, you inform them about the wonders that your items deliver (your solution or core magnet—why they should be attracted to what you've got or what's in it for them).

The problem is that people don't listen. They've been bombarded with so much advertising, so many sales pitches, offers and promises that they've shut their ears. When they see billboards, ads or commercials, they don't register. They rarely notice what a company is selling what and if they do, they quickly forget.

Most people ignore promotions. They don't pay attention; to them, it's just more noise or static.

The traditional approaches such as mass advertising no longer work very effectively. They tend to be expensive and don't produce great results.

If you want to create more interest and generate sales, you have to attract potential consumers in other, more innovative ways.

Until recently, the alternatives were slim and the deck was stacked against the little guys. The four main TV networks and a handful of media giants controlled the airways and print. Since they charged a fortune, small companies could only afford to deal locally or buy postage-stamp sized national ads. For a time, telemarketing and direct mail had their day, but they overdid it, they called too often and clogged our mailboxes, which spelled their doom.

QUICK STEPS: *FOCUS ON GETTING AND KEEPING YOUR CUSTOMERS' ATTENTION.*

In the past, the focus was on getting people to take action and, more specifically, to convince them to buy. Today, the focus is more on getting their attention. Since we're now overloaded with information, everyone has less time. So getting potential customers' attention has become the top priority. Once you have their attention, you have to hold their interest.

Permission Marketing

In 1999, Seth Godin wrote his seminal book *Permission Marketing.* In it, he recommended that businesses create ongoing relationships with potential customers. By creating these relationships, potential customers would become more comfortable with you and be more open to buying from you in the future. Godin suggested that businesses lay the groundwork for future sales by engaging potential customers in dialogs and interactive relationships.

By building relationships with potential customers, businesses could make sure that they didn't get bypassed when the potential customers decided to buy.

According to Godin, the process should be continual so that the relationships grow stronger over the years. By maintaining these relationships—keeping your customers engaged—you can find out and keep abreast of what your customers want and how to provide it. Continual contact can also help your business avoid having your offerings commoditized because customers value your input if it is relevant and gets them closer to reaching their goals.

Your potential customers benefit because you offer them items that they need and value. Remember, your customers are also flattered when they believe that their opinions are considered and are in fact important to their suppliers. Relationships build your customers' loyalty.

"A business can now ask a consumer directly if he would like more information," Goden points out. "A business can now reward a consumer for receiving and acknowledging its message, insuring that the consumers' own interest is served by learning about a new product or service."

Your business should ask your customers what they need and what they think they might need in the future. Top marketers and salespeople involve their customers in the planning process. They act like an advisory member of their customers' team.

Once you establish a relationship, you must keep the relationship strong. This is similar to starting and keeping a friendship going. If your customers like and benefit from the relationship (friendship), they will put their trust in you and your business. You will become their favorite and they will support you by continuing to buy your products and recommending them to others.

Think of Oprah or Ellen DeGeneres. You tune them in because you like what they have to say and the relationship you feel you have with them. This goes back to the *American Idol* model and the Performance Economy. You are in the entertainment, attention/ratings business. If your show is boring, you are not going to attract viewers or an audience.

Google is really a popularity ranking service that sells ads (AdWords) to the most popular companies' shows. The most popular person or company on a Google results page gets the most free audience or traffic. For example, let's say you sell dog training. When customers search the internet by typing in the keywords "dog training," the top-ranked company or person offering dog training gets a lot of free viewers—40% of the traffic— on the first results page.

This means the most popular—those that get the most attention (traffic)—benefit over everyone else.

In addition, Google sells ads to advertisers who want to advertise to people searching for certain keywords or information, in this example, dog training. This is the main source of Google's billions of revenues. They are the arbiter of whose information is most popular, relevant and of highest quality and thus, who gets the most attention.

Note that attracting attention is the first step in the formula that Madison Avenue has long used in advertising. That formula is AIDA:

- A = Attention
- I = Interest
- D = Desire
- A = Action

Performance Marketing

Permission marketing is how you attract customers to your business.

You need to get their permission to enter into a relationship with you. This is critical on the Internet since it is against the law to market—email—someone directly without their permission (what is called "spam"). That is why Internet marketers offer free information in exchange for someone's email address or permission to get in touch with them.

Performance marketing is how you sell your goods or services once you receive permission. You get customers' business because you show them that your items perform excellently, that they deliver what customers want. You give them free stuff so they can test drive what you are offering and be open to buy your paid stuff.

In the Performance Economy, you're always onstage. Whether you're online, off-line, on the phone or face-to-face, it's your show and you must be the star along with your products and services. Millions of others, people and businesses, are in the wings just dying to compete with you. They are willing to do anything to get their chance—including destroying you.

QUICK STEPS: *GIVE CONSTANT VALUE TO YOUR AUDIENCE TO KEEP THEM TUNED IN.*

After you have their attention, your challenge is to keep them tuned in. You still must enthrall them because at any stage, they can always switch you off. You have to make it good, give it your best shot, because it may be the only chance you get.

> **QUICK STEPS:** *KEEP THE DIALOGUE GOING*
> *TO MAINTAIN ENGAGEMENT OF YOUR AUDIENCE.*
>
> Keeping a dialogue going is called engagement. Engagement cements relationships and forges bonds. It's the glue with which empires are built.

Jimmy points out, "When I started this business, I was on my phone all day long, every day, all day talking to people. Relationships. I'm in the people business. It should be called relationship marketing."

The ability to engage through communication, collaboration, education and entertainment is the essence of face-to-face networking, social networking and direct selling alike.

Social networking is what you do on Facebook, YouTube, MySpace and LinkedIn. Social networking is very similar to what you do in direct selling—you engage friends, family and business associates.

Networking itself in any of its forms, especially online and via cell phones, enables you to spread the word and multiply your market penetration because you can reach so many more people at one time (it creates leverage—a small effort, such as sending out emails in multiples, generates a much larger response).

Direct selling at its core is leveraging networks of people who spread the word and spread the distribution of products that no one person on their own could do. That's the essence of leverage. With technology, direct selling and social networking properly combined create enormous leverage.

Social Networking

Why is social networking so important? It is a way to get attention, build audience awareness, and create dialogue and engagement.

You do social networking every day. You get in touch with friends and share stuff like a movie you liked or a new great restaurant. So, how do you properly go about networking in the world of the Internet, cell phones and other technologies?

First, position yourself.

Join communities where people will want to engage with you and be open to what you say. Once you become an accepted part of a network or community, your voice will carry more weight if they believe you are authentic and your comments and advice help them. As you become more accepted, be a leader and become the magnet, not just another me-too. People will naturally be drawn to you as a leader. At this point, they will be more open to your telling them about what you are selling. It's the same approach as giving free goods to get people comfortable with who you are and what you stand for.

Your social network is a warm market because it's made up of people with whom you have a relationship—even if that relationship is just that you're in the same social network. When you're in a social network, it gives you leverage. It provides you with the power (leverage) to reach masses of people with one message or contact—one click on a send button. It gives you the reach that until recently was only available to the largest businesses.

QUICK STEPS: *SEEK LEVERAGE IN EVERYTHING YOU DO.*

To get leverage, integrate the Internet, cell phones and technology. Become a magnet by making people comfortable and proving yourself and then start marketing. Build rapport so that they are willing to listen to what you say about your goods and services.

Like social networking, direct selling is fundamentally people-oriented. It is about personal relationships. People like to be involved with and buy from those they like.

That happens to be Jimmy's secret to success in network marketing. Jimmy builds relationships and rapport first. He never sells. Once they are comfortable with him, and he has their permission, he lays out the opportunity and lets people choose to buy.

Jimmy revealed his winning 3-Step Formula to marketing and sales success. To attract customers through the Internet, **Jimmy says:** "First, I call you up, I contact you, I make an appointment for you to either meet me on the phone and we both get on the website. Second, I let you go to the website either by yourself or with me." The final step is to ask the magic question: "Is this something you'd be interested in doing? Do you see yourself doing this? Is this a product that you think would benefit you? Do you think there's a business opportunity here that you might be interested in?"

That is how you can benefit from technology. It is the way you can compete with Coca-Cola. You can learn to make people comfortable with you. You can show them, if you pick the right products, why what you're selling is best for them. And you can use your cell phone and your company's website to leverage the amount of people you contact. That's what direct selling is all about.

The Top Reasons Why People Fail

Most people fail in business because they:

1. Think small
2. ..... Fail to accurately calculate their chances to succeed
3. Focus too much on short-term rewards
4. Don't build a solid foundation
5. Have bad timing. They get in too early or too late
6. Choose the wrong industry
7. Pick the wrong company
8. Select the wrong compensation/payment plan

When I reflect on my career, I see that when one of my ventures failed, it was rarely due to the product or the industry. Usually, it was because of the people involved. They were:

1. Either dishonest, incompetent, or both
2. Great at selling a vision, but not at implementing it
3. Able to implement their visions, but they were dishonest
4. Didn't want other people to reap the rewards from their investments. They couldn't control their greed

7

Leveraging

You've been reading about leverage, which is getting multiples on your input or effort using technology or other's resources.

Leverage is the secret that underlies all wealth.

You cannot do it all yourself, nor can you get really wealthy on hourly wages. Jimmy could not make a fraction of what he makes being a butcher. His average salary over 40 years was $10,000 ($400,000 over 40 years), and now he makes $15,000 in a day or 50% more in one day than he made in a year! Jimmy put it this way: "I would have to work 200 years as a butcher to earn what I earned last year in Isagenix®. I would have to work 2,000 years as a butcher to earn what my family has earned in the past seven years, which is $20 million dollars."

Now what greater example and proof of leverage and wealth building? And Jimmy started at 74 years old with Isagenix®.

This is why I am focusing so much on leverage. You need to understand this up-front, just as Jimmy did when he realized the power of people, network marketing and leverage: "The numbers jumped out. The mathematics of network marketing jumped out at me."

The easiest way to understand leverage is to look at how you open a can of paint. Since the lid fits under the outer rim, you can't open the can with your fingers. You must insert a tool like a screwdriver to pry open the top. So you place the flat part of the screwdriver blade on an angel between the lid and the rim, and push down on the handle of the screwdriver to force open the top.

Without the screwdriver you cannot open the can of paint. With a screwdriver and little effort, you can open it. That's mechanical leverage.

Let's look at another example. If your car has 300 horsepower, when you hit the gas, your car will go faster than a car that only has 100 horsepower—even though in both situations you are applying essentially the same amount of pressure to the accelerator. So the 300 horsepower car gives you better leverage.

Remember the 1% rule that I introduced you to in Chapter 3. Only 1% of every 100 people will become rich. That 1% also controls the lion's share—20% of world earnings (20x what the average person makes and 30x the average person's wealth). Again, 20x and 30x the average person is astounding. The primary factor that put them on top is leverage. They had the same amount of time as everyone else; however, it's what they did in that time that made the difference. They didn't just trade their time to make money; they made the best use of their time by applying leverage.

Warren Buffett is considered to be the greatest investor of all time. He has used leverage to build his fabulous wealth. Buffett got investors to invest their money with him, then took that money and invested it. Not only did Buffett make money on those investments, but he also received a percentage of the profits that his investors made.

People Leveraging

Borrowing money is just one form of leverage. Leverage can also be making use of other people's talent, their knowledge, their skills and technology, to create assets. We call this people leveraging.

People leveraging increases with more and more people. If you have 500 people selling your customized photo albums, you usually can profit more than if you only have five people selling them.

People leveraging is the key to social networking and direct selling. It's having an army, not one or two people, working for you, selling your goods or championing your cause. It's utilizing all of their many talents for your benefit. By working with others' resources, such as their time, contacts and expertise, you have many more people-hours working for you.

In direct selling, leveraging means growing your downline, the group of distributors you recruit. It's simply having more people selling your goods.

Positive Leverage

This is where the more people you have selling, the more money you make.

In financial terms, when you borrow money, you make money on the money you borrow as well as your own.

If I can get a 10% return on $1,000, I will get a $100 return.

If I borrow $800 at 5%, then I only have to invest $200 of my own money.

If I pay $40 on the debt, I make $60 net of my debt expense ($100 — $40 = $60).

My $60 is my net return on my $200 investment or 30% ($60/$200).

I went from 10% to 30% because I borrowed money at 5% and got 10% coming in.

Leverage also has a downside. We call it negative leverage and here is how it works.

Assume that you borrowed $1,000 at 5% interest and invest it. However, instead of getting a 10% return, you only get a 1% return. Your actual income is $10 (instead of $100 that we got in the positive leverage example), which is $30 less than the amount of interest you have to pay (800 x 5% = $40 interest — $10 income = $30 loss). That $30 loss must come out of your pocket.

Negative leverage was a major cause of the recent Great Recession. It is also one of the major reasons why people don't build wealth. Instead of building assets, they build up debt. They incur expenses and liabilities with their homes, cars, credit cards and student loans. They have little income, as in this negative leverage example, and lots of debt, causing them to lose money or just hang on. They dig themselves into a deep financial hole and many never get out.

They also dream small. They don't dream huge. Their focus is making income and making it quick. They don't build assets first.

Build Assets

As I said in Chapter 3, to achieve financial freedom, you must build assets. In direct selling, the ultimate goal is to build a large downline that will keep earning money for you. That is your major asset, your Golden Goose. If you have a downline comprised of many distributors, they will pay you steadily (Golden Eggs), like clockwork, every week.

We are now witnessing the convergence of many factors that never previously existed. There is more opportunity now to use leverage in the form of social networking and direct selling and create substantial wealth faster than ever before.

If you have valuable assets in place, you can market and leverage them virtually anywhere. Through the Internet, entrepreneurs who dare to dream huge have a larger and more level playing field. Those who wish to succeed now have a better chance of doing so because technology enables them to engage many more people. With one click of a send button, their message can reach thousands, even millions. Through virtual worlds, they can engage people everywhere as easily as they can engage just one.

With all this available to you and others, why are so many struggling and why do so few have assets?

It comes down to mind-set. Those who succeed learn to see patterns and opportunities that others don't. They train by study and trial and error how to take advantage of opportunities and find the resources they don't have (leverage). Go get my free special report called "Mastering the Art of Leverage." Here's the link: **http://www.masteringtheartofleverage.com/**

8

Dare to Dream HUGE!

Entrepreneurs succeed because they dare to dream huge, as Malcolm Gladwell wrote in his article in the *New Yorker*. Entrepreneurs have a different mind-set than small business people. They want to grow something large, they want to assemble resources and build them into great growth companies.

On the surface, entrepreneurs are viewed as high risk-takers. In reality, however, they're always looking to reduce their downside risk while they keep their upside returns high. True entrepreneurs succeed because they are always positioning themselves, so the odds weigh in their favor.

Gladwell went on, "The risk-taking model suggests that the entrepreneur's chief advantage is one of temperament—*he's braver than the rest of us*. In the predator model, the entrepreneur's advantage is analytical—he's better at figuring out a sure thing than the rest of us.*"

But you won't find it if you don't think that you will find a sure thing in the first place. What's going to motivate you to do all this work and defer instant gratification? You need something big enough to keep your own attention and keep you committed and engaged.

That is why you have to dream huge, on an epic scale, or else you won't be a huge success. You can have all the know-how, put in all the work, but never get to the top thinking small. To make it big, think bigger than big, think huge.

What does this type of thinking do? It electrifies the mind—not only your mind, but the minds of others.

What do you lose to dream more than big, to dream huge, gigantically? Nothing! Show the world that you believe in yourself and what you are doing. Tell them about your big dreams and let them see how convinced you are that they will come true.

Jimmy dreamed huge. They thought he was nuts. Ray Kroc dreamed huge when he first spoke to the McDonald brothers. Most thought he was crazy. Same with Colonel Sanders with Kentucky Fried Chicken, Wally Amos of Famous Amos and Debbie Fields of Mrs. Fields.

Now does this mean you just dream huge and that's it? Of course not. That's why I am showing you the steps to turn your huge dream into a reality. It is my passion to help you make your dreams come true. Who doesn't like to see a newborn baby come into the world and soon take its first steps and grow into a beautiful successful child and adult? That's what I love too. New dreams are like newborns—great ideas that blossom into magnificent realities.

Inner Confidence

When you lack great inner confidence, others can tell. Right off the bat, they can spot it a mile away. They know it and many of them won't want to be associated with you. Most will avoid you like the plague.

Business success is built on leadership, stepping up front and taking control. It takes guts and moxie. Top network marketers exude confidence and are bold. They know their goods and services, their companies, their people, their plans and potential inside out. They're also experts who are passionate about their products and services. People are drawn to them.

Jimmy Smith told me, "I was a dreamer. I've been a dreamer all my life and I had to make a decision. It was: Am I going to shrink my income to live on my pension or increase my income to live my dreams? I chose the latter."

Jimmy dared to dream huge. Here's his recipe for making it huge:

1. Have a huge dream.

2. Make a full commitment to fulfill your dream and make it a reality.

3. Dare to:

   a. Believe fully

   b. Be courageous

   c. Make a leap of faith

Dreaming huge—setting the loftiest goals—will motivate you and drive you to overcome the obstacles, problems and constraints that you will inevitably face.

Small thinkers in network marketing say, "I am going to become a network marketer to make an extra $250, $500 or $1,000 per month." They usually miss their targets. Most never consistently reach their small goals, and they end up frustrated, disillusioned and with far less than they hoped.

Shoot for the stars. Usually, it takes just about the same effort. When you dream huge, your initial successes will motivate you. It will drive you to bring in more and more.

Follow Jimmy Smith's example. He told himself, "I'm going to be a millionaire." And he did many, many times over.

And the good news is: So can you!

Just understand, at first you are not going to feel comfortable thinking this way. It's probably alien. You may have thought big from time to time. Then the inner critic popped up and said, "Who are you kidding? Forget it. You don't have a chance. The top people were born that way. The top people had the right connections. They got the money genes. Entrepreneurs are born not made."

This is true, right?

Sorry. Wrong.

Keep reading.

What I am going to reveal to you about the belief that entrepreneurs are born, not nurtured, will be shocking and will rock your boat!

9

Born or Learned?

People constantly find reasons not to act. They look for the perfect time to make the entrepreneurial leap when in reality there is no perfect time to leap—ever.

For every opportunity, they'll give you a list of why it just can't work. Each answer, every excuse, moves them further from where they actually want to be.

Most of their reasons are simply not true. For example, many don't plunge into direct selling because they don't feel they have the right pedigree, the right upbringing, the right education, the right street smarts or the right resources. All their lives they've heard that marketers are born not made, and they've bought that myth.

Nonsense!

You can learn to be a big success. Untold thousands have. You don't have to be born to wealth to acquire it. You just have to want it…really want it.

In a study of entrepreneurs led by Vivek Wadhwa, a visiting scholar at the University of California at Berkeley, a senior research associate at Harvard Law School and Director of Research at the Center for Entrepreneurship, Wadhwa wrote, "Entrepreneurs aren't born, they're made, and they aren't anything like you think they are. My team surveyed 549 successful entrepreneurs. We found that the majority didn't have entrepreneurial parents; they didn't have entrepreneurial aspirations while they were going to school. They simply got tired of working for others, had a great idea they wanted to commercialize or woke up one day with an urgent desire to build wealth before they retired."

Wadhwa's study revealed that 52% of successful entrepreneurs were the first members of their immediate families to build businesses. He lists as examples: Bill Gates, Jeff Bezos, Larry Page, Sergey Brin and Russell Simmons.

The study found: "No significant difference in the success factors or hurdles faced by entrepreneurs who were extremely interested in entrepreneurship in school and [those] who were likely to set up the lemonade stands and the ones who lacked interest."

According to Wadhwa, a number of influential business commentators "make quick judgments about people based on the stereotypes in their minds." These stereotypes are not only frequently wrong, but they also perpetuate the fable that business superstars are born, not made.

The Big Difference

Education is the difference, not genetics, Wadhwa's study reported. "Education provided a huge advantage, but there wasn't a big difference between firms founded by Ivy League graduates and graduates of other universities."

However, entrepreneurs with college educations significantly outperformed those who were not as well educated. Since we now live in a knowledge-based economy that requires more technological skills, the study's conclusion about the pivotal role of education makes absolute sense.

QUICK STEPS: *THE RIGHT EDUCATION*
IS THE ROAD TO RICHES.

Here's the approach you should take. Even though I have an MBA from Columbia University, my real education came from being in the trenches. The role of education in generating success goes even further when it's born out of determination and drive. You need a purpose and a passion to drive you to educate yourself, dream huge and build a great business.

Those who truly want to be the best, study and learn. They become sponges who soak up everything in their field and fields related to theirs. They are constantly on the prowl, looking for new and better information. It becomes second nature to them, and they can't stop.

The top people understand the importance of education and how it helped them succeed. It's inexorably connected to who they are, what they do and what they want to become. It's as much a part of them as one of their limbs.

Dispel Myths of Your Obstacles

To make a difference and get ahead, you must constantly assess opinions that you may be relying upon.

A fabulous way to make your name—to get attention—is to bust myths. Show that something everyone has always accepted is just not so. If you can relate it to business, you can make a fortune.

Next, carry myth busting forward into your own life. You can make a fortune by doing this as well.

Here's how.

Examine the reasons why you aren't doing or achieving all you want. Make a list and identify everything that is holding you back—your obstacles and constraints. Then try to assess it honestly.

When you examine your list, ask yourself if your reasons are really true. Take each one and ask yourself: is your obstacle valid or is it one you invented subconsciously to hold yourself back?

If your reason doesn't make sense when you really question it, rebut it with sound logic.. Every time your excuse or myth comes into your mind, you must reject it by having an internal debate. Imagine in your mind the way you have to act with this reason or excuse out of the way and begin to act accordingly. You may feel awkward or uncomfortable. That is expected. But soon you will see improvement, if not immediately.

However, if you find that you had a valid reason, not to move on, try to find alternatives that you can pursue. Don't stop or quit; find other ways to reach your goal.

Don't hold back or say you can't.

Jimmy chose an excellent company in Isagenix®. He placed a bet and went for it. He could have stayed where he was. He had built up a very respectable income at his latest network marketing firm. Yet he wanted more. He took a leap of faith even when others thought he had lost it.

Again, examine things you always relied upon as the truth. Sometimes, the belief you always thought to be true may be false. Change this one belief and your entire outlook changes for the better. Do you think you can't possibly speak in public? What was the last time you tried? You weren't born that way, and you can grow to be another person entirely. So go ahead. Take the plunge.

10
Why the Internet?

Let's look at why the Internet and social media are the areas to focus on if you want to build a profitable network marketing business.

Here's a fact that can change the way you approach your business: "The Network Marketing Association reports that face-to-face selling makes up 77% of all sales, with the majority of those taking place in someone's home." (*Success from Home* magazine, May, 2010).

Now we'll add a rule you may have heard: the 80/20 rule. In business, the rule of thumb is that 80% of your sales come from 20% of your clients. Originally, the rule derived from an Italian economist, Vilfredo Pareto, who observed in 1906 that 20% of Italy's population controlled 80% of its wealth.

Based on Pareto's Principle, the 80/20 Rule, you should focus 80% of your time and energy on the 20% of your work that is vital or really important. Another way to say this is to not only "work smart" but work smart on the right things.

Another way to view the 80/20 rule is to look at where 77% (almost 80%) of network marketers are spending their time—face-to-face selling. But where's the big opportunity? In completely different fields than face-to-face selling, such as through the Internet (the other 20%).

You want to look at what your competition is doing and add more possibilities.

Baseball Hall of Famer Willie Keeler responded when asked how he hit so consistently for a high batting average: "Hit 'em where they ain't." To succeed in business, you have to do something different. Yes, a lot of people are using the Internet. But most network marketers are not using it to their advantage. They are using it simply as a tool to initiate, perform transactions and track transactions.

Used correctly, the Internet can give you the edge if you can harness its power.

Some people are reluctant to do business on the Internet. They prefer to deal directly with their customers, go on sales calls and deal face-to-face or by phone. They may feel uncomfortable with technology and fear that they will never get up to speed—so they avoid it.

Sadly, while they stock up on carbon paper, business is passing them by. E-commerce, business on the Internet, is a multi-trillion dollar industry— the biggest marketplace in history. Economically, Internet commerce may be the only viable route you can pursue because most new business systems are being created for the Internet. Before long, virtually all elements of the business process will have moved to the Internet because it is so efficient, cost-effective and pervasive. Soon, virtually all business will be done online.

Customers, potential distributors and whomever you want to reach is on the Internet. The Internet is where the action is. It just makes sense to *fish where the fish are biting.*

You should realize that using computers these days is easy. A lot of people are computer phobic, yet the technology is becoming so simple. Jimmy Smith started using it at the age of 74. He evolved into computers because now the tools are so easy to use that people of any age coming into direct selling shouldn't be worried about technology.

Doing business on the Internet will put you with the players, the movers and shakers who are building the new business frontiers. They're laying the foundation, and tomorrow all elements of business will be structured and transacted on it. By doing business on the Internet, you will be honing your skills and learning the new strategies you will need in the years ahead.

Just as email and texting replaced postal mail and phone calls, websites are replacing face-to-face meetings. Websites have already replaced brochures, catalogs, spec sheets, price lists and order forms. Automation now can do much of what you previously had to spend face-to-face time on. That means you can work more productively and lucratively.

Using the power of a computer can extend your downline effortlessly. Jimmy has an incredible downline of 400,000 people, but he can bring any of them up on his computer at a moment's notice. He can tell you what every single person bought last week, how much they made, how many times they cycled, how many people they sponsored, what they're doing or not doing. He knows everything on his computer. That's important when you're moving $2 million dollars worth of product every week wholesale.

Jimmy never sees or touches any product or any money. Corporate takes care of all of that. They calculate the cycles, they pay everybody, they send out emails.

Jimmy can contact anybody in his organization through email, phone calls and text messages. He has people in Hong Kong, Taiwan, Australia, New Zealand. It's an international, worldwide business. He gets paid from those people in Australia or Hong Kong, people he's never met and may never meet.

This is the 21st century and you'll be either online or in the bread line. You can do everything on the Internet.

Jimmy laughs about his global reach: "I called a fellow in Florida to order a hundred books and send them out to people. I got a text message back saying, 'I'm in China doing a seminar. I'll be back next week. Call Sandy, she'll take care of you.'

"I texted him back saying, 'Okay, thanks, pal. Travel safe. Talk to you next week.' I thought to myself that I call Florida, I get a text from China, I text back. I'm talking to somebody in China. It's amazing."

QUICK STEPS: *THE GREATEST TOOL TO EXECUTE LEVERAGE.*

The Internet—other than your mind—is the greatest tool to execute leverage. You can reach so many with relatively little effort. Even though the Internet has been around for a while, it is constantly evolving. This innovative medium provides numerous ways to connect, collaborate, communicate, educate and entertain your clients.

What makes direct selling so attractive as a business model is that it functions in many ways like social media, where people communicate, collaborate, educate and entertain each other.

To get ahead of the pack, read books on social media such as *Trust Agents* by Chris Brogan and Julien Smith. Similar to Jimmy Smith's view, they make this point about the Internet and social media: "There are people out there right now working to understand these new technologies and learning how to use them—from etiquette to audience building and beyond. They are learning the ropes. They are the pioneers, mastering the latest one-to-many communications methods. Like your kids, they know more about technology, and maybe even more about people, than you do; and that makes them very powerful. We call them trust agents."

Whether you or I like it or not, you have to change with the times like Jimmy did and keeps doing—you need to learn the ropes.

Expanded Customer Base

Here's what's so exciting about the Internet and social media once you learn the ropes.

The Internet allows you to reach infinitely more potential customers. In the virtual world, you're no longer geographically limited.

From your home, you can call upon the same or similar resources as multinational corporations, industry giants. You can have access to similar equipment, vendors and subcontractors. Like the largest, most powerful manufacturers, even the smaller market networker can design a product, send the design and specifications to China, and receive a prototype and cost quotes.

When customers like your goods or services, they will recommend you to others. Referrals are great leverage since someone is introducing you or solidifying a relationship for you using their good will and influence. This is what occurs every second on the Internet. The same happens in the offline world, but on the Internet, referrals can be made public such as on LinkedIn. This form of advertising can be very powerful.

Another way to leverage on the Internet is by using testimonials. Customers will also give you testimonials that you can post on your website. Testimonials are advertisements and recommendations that influence potential customers' decisions. A sure-fire way to make money on the Internet is having customers praising you and stating that your goods or services are second to none.

The late famous network marketing guru Gary Halbert told a group that he was addressing, "If you went into the hamburger business, what one thing would you want to differentiate your business from everyone else?" His audience told him location, a great system, the best-tasting hamburger, the best-priced burger, great fries, gorgeous waitresses, a fabulous visual environment and a great experience.

With each answer, the guru kept shaking his head no. Finally, he told them the right answer: "The deciding factor I would want most is customers who are starving. I want starving customers."

The Internet has the starving customers. It's filled with people who want to buy. Many are browsing the Internet just because they want to buy.

Potential customers log on to find goods and services; they are hungry and will willingly pay if you have what they crave.

On the Internet, you can take your items and then match them with customers who are starving for your goods. And when you post information about your goods or services, many customers will come to you. The Internet facilitates the convergence of supply and demand: you have an item that customers need, and the Internet is where you come together and make sales.

Focus on selling to the right people. Identify who they are and then shape your campaign for them. See if they are in communities that you can approach.

Let's take an example I used earlier where you have a dog training product you want to sell. You want to target people typing the words "dog training" into their searches on Google, Bing, Yahoo and other search engines. You have to decide, are you going to give dog training tips, classes, collars, leashes or fences? Each word—keyword—you use on your website can change your target audience. A keyword is a word you place in your text, often near the beginning, that a search engine such as Google can then find. It often is the bold word in the short description under the search results. So, using the right keyword, are you going to position yourself as a dog training expert or a dog obedience trainer?

As you can see, your offer and potential revenue can turn on a word or two. That's the power and leverage of the Internet. You can reach so many people so quickly and target them specifically. The Internet can expand the number of people in your downline faster than any tool ever used in direct selling.

11

How Direct Selling
Leads to Riches

Let's take a closer look at what makes direct selling a powerful business model that can lead to massive fortunes when you take the right steps.

Direct selling is a way of selling goods or services through groups or networks of people. By marketing through networks, these companies can operate on enormous scales and deeply penetrate more markets. Instead of sending one or two salespeople into a given territory, direct selling saturates markets by sending lots of people to sell in many areas.

The success of direct selling comes from geometric rather than linear growth, as I've pointed out already. Let's review these concepts, since they are at the core of determining financial success

First, let's look at linear growth. If you work ten hours and are paid at a certain rate for every hour you work, you receive ten times the hourly rate. If that rate is $10, you will earn $100 or ten times the hourly rate.

Geometric growth gives you greater leverage than linear growth. You get more from the same or slightly greater effort—see the example below.

Now, let's look at how direct selling works and how geometric growth applies.

Direct selling enables you to bring more people on board, and they give your goods and services greater market saturation. For example, if your company has two salespeople and they sign up two more, you immediately double your sales force. If those four each sign two more and each of them sign another two, the four grow to 16, 32, 64 and so on.

Linear growth: 2 people + 2 people + 2 people + 2 people + 2 people + 2 people = <u>12 people</u>

Geometric growth: 2 people x 2 people x 2 people x 2 people x 2 people x 2 people = <u>64 people</u>

Traditional sales organizations hire salespeople, and most pay them commissions on what the people sell. Direct selling companies also have salespeople, who are called distributors. Direct selling companies give their distributors commissions on what they sell AND they also give their distributors commissions on sales made by distributors they have recruited. They also receive sales from distributors that their distributors have recruited and so on. How much network marketers or distributors are paid is based upon what is called the direct selling company's compensation plan.

So it stands to reason that you can make much more if, with basically the same effort, you can have 64 people selling your wares rather than just 12.

Jimmy understood the power of leverage and geometric growth. He felt that the concept was quite basic. The more you share, the more you lead and teach others:

- The more distributors and customers you will enroll
- The more satisfied your distributors and customers are the more money you make.

He saw network marketing as a family-like undertaking, so he brought in his own family. Now Jimmy has enlarged his family to 400,000 distributors—adding 400 per day and growing—who are loyal to him and Isagenix®.

WARNING: *Networking marketing is not a get-rich-quick scheme! Like any other business, it takes a lot of time, effort, planning and hard work.*

The image of direct selling has been tarnished because a number of direct selling companies have emphasized getting rich quickly. As a result, they attract impatient, greedy people who do not want to put in the time and effort needed to succeed.

Yet direct selling is essentially a sound business if it is approached like any other business. One 24-year-old joined Isagenix®, then Facebook, and in a month, got 30 people to sign up to his downline. Another person in Jimmy's downline reportedly made $13,500 a week after only a year.

Direct selling does work if you know how to find key distributors. Sure, an element of luck is involved, but direct selling, like any business, is hard work, especially up-front, but once you get rolling, you can do exceptionally well.

Downlines

Throughout this book I use the term "downline." In direct selling, your downline consists of the people you recruit to be distributors. You receive a commission on the goods and services that the distributors in your downline sell to customers and the sales produced by the distributors that they recruit.

You teach the people in your downline and help them because you get a cut of their sales. Downlines are how network-marketing companies build huge sales forces and how you can make your fortune.

Your upline consists of the sponsor who recruited you into the network-marketing company and the people who sponsored them. The people in your upline mentor you, teach you about the company and show you the ropes. They get a share of everything and everyone you and your downline sell and recruit.

As you can see, direct selling is a people business. People need people to make money. In direct selling, people create the geometric growth and leverage that no one person can do alone. Go get my free special report called "Mastering the Art of Leverage." Here's the link: **http://www. Masteringtheartofleverage.com/** or **www.StepsTo.com**

Cooperation

In the overall scheme of things, no matter what is taught, some people will earn more than others. Their success can usually be attributed to dedication, time, money and resources—and some luck.

Here's a proven fact: cooperation gives everyone a better chance of succeeding.

Cooperation tends to work better than competition.

Some more facts: Did you know that cooperation helps:

1. Businesspeople earn higher salaries

2. Students get higher grades

3. Scientists have more articles published

4. Increase creativity

5. Improve health

6. People feel more in control of their lives

According to University of Minnesota Professor Roger T. Johnson, "People learn best when they work best with each other."

However, too much cooperation has its downside. It can lead to group-think, yes-man syndrome and conformity.

QUICK STEPS: *YOUR BASE.*

To build and expand your base, or downline, learn to lead others and promote cooperation and collaboration—not competition. By

---

nature, human beings seek leaders. They want to find people who can show them how they can make life better.

Cooperation can also be contagious because most people like working in teams. When they work that way, they can accomplish more and their success can be sweeter; they can share it with more people.

Going though a cooperative group experience builds friendships, cements bonds and provides long-lasting memories.

Cooperation in Network Marketing

In network marketing, you share information and develop personal and professional contacts. You are rewarded for sharing information that results in product sales. Network marketing empowers you to build your own networking sales organization from your personal and professional contacts, which also empowers everyone to do the same, creating exponential growth of your network. You can earn income from the successful efforts of your network of business associates. Unlike conventional corporations with one chief executive at the top, in network marketing everyone is the CEO of his or her own independent organization.

A network marketing company supplies the product. Then they join in a partnership with a network of independent representatives, each one in business for themselves. The company takes care of the research and development, finances, management, public relations, production, warehousing, packaging, quality control, administration, shipping, data processing, the accounting and payment of representative sales commission checks.

Unlike in traditional business, career advancement in network marketing comes directly from helping to create success with those that you introduce to the company. Network marketing is sharing information that results in product sales. (Source: internetnextstep.com)

12
Social Networks

The key to business is distribution—getting both your message and your products or services out. To succeed in business, consumers have to hear about your items in order to buy them. The first step is to reach potential customers and let them know that your goods exist.

To repeat, the problem is that people don't listen. Attention is at a super premium. Every waking second people are pitching you because there are more sellers than buyers. You see billboards, ads or commercials everywhere you go until it no longer registers. You hardly notice what a company is selling you, and if you do, you quickly forget because there are always more offers and promotions. Why would you pay attention? It's just more noise.

Traditional approaches no longer work well. They tend to be expensive and don't produce great results.

QUICK STEPS: *MY RECURRENT THEME.*

If you want to create more interest and generate sales, you must attract potential consumers **in other ways.**

This is why I am advocating combining the power of the Internet and using different advertising strategies that use Google AdWords, Facebook Ads and social media. It is more important to understand the strategies since specific tactics change so quickly. We will cover more techniques later, but the emphasis should be on strategies. These will be long-lasting, such as how to build trust in an environment where everyone has such a lack of trust of politicians, bankers and businesspeople.

New Developments

To create the best strategies, you need to look at the big picture and how we've gotten to where we are.

Recently, developments in the world of media made a quantum leap. First, cable TV arrived and brought us scores of specialized new channels. Cable channels covered all the bases. They zeroed in on every language, race and demographic; every sport, hobby, interest, trend and point of view. Cable TV finally gave advertisers affordable alternatives to the networks and frequently provided a better value.

Following cable, the Internet explosion occurred. It opened everything more. At first, the Internet marketed directly through websites. Sellers put up sites to sell their wares. Sites could reach people all over the world. So from their kitchen, local merchants in Topeka could expand into markets all over the globe. Plus, they could target specific groups of potential buyers and hold back and forth dialogs with them.

Now computers, the Internet, iPads, cell phones and the like now let you instantly contact someone. These technologies are enabling us to spawn a new species of communities, online communities, that we call social networks.

Social networks are composed of people who have similar interests and who want to connect. Like our forbearers who decided to gather together in caves, people today join social networks for human interaction. Today, they tweet and exchange ideas. Social networkers tell each other about goods and services and how they feel about them. And since they're in communities of like-minded individuals, their opinions carry great weight.

MySpace, Facebook and YouTube are the main sites. People join social networking communities to socialize with friends and those with similar interests. Social networking is based on friendships: one friend tells another friend who tells another friend and so on. Friends tell friends about their networks and their interests. In the process, some people become more popular and make new friends. They build larger pages and attract bigger followings.

If you or one of your Facebook friends hear about a certain product and recommend it on Facebook, that recommendation could potentially be communicated to thousands, even millions, of people. The recommendation will be trusted and boost the item's sales.

Let me give you an example. Let's say that I have been in a social network for a while and have forged a number of strong relationships. Then I'm introduced to a business opportunity that simply amazes me. In my excitement, I mention it to my social network friends and we talk about it.

What happens? If I am respected by the community, then my recommendation will influence others in the community to take note and take action. What I have that is so valuable is the community's attention. I am at the center of the power structure of that community and possibly others as well.

QUICK STEPS: *BUILD YOUR RELATIONSHIPS AND RESPECT FIRST.*

The key to your success in a social network is to build your relationships and respect first—not sell. Jump at the opportunity to get to know people online, give them knowledge of where to get resources and reach the right people when they need access. In the social network world, people skills are immensely valuable.

Social networking and direct selling have much in common. Both need to enlist newcomers so they can expand and prosper. And their growth must be strong and steady.

To succeed, both rely heavily on the skill of their people to recruit new members.

The skills that make successful social networkers are essentially the same as those of top network marketers. So it stands to reason that people who are successful social networkers will also excel at direct selling—and vice versa.

Now, let's look at the two most significant differences.

Social networking is primarily a social tool. Its major purpose is to bring people together. Business and moving goods is not its main objective. Dedicated business sites like LinkedIn are the exception.

However, members of social networks have influence. So if, in their interchanges, they mention goods and services, commercial benefits slip in through the back door. Since social networking sites are visited by billions of people, that back door is humongous.

In contrast, direct selling groups are businesses that exist to make money. Their primary purpose is to sell goods and services through the network and to extend the direct selling group's reach.

- In social networking, members are basically saying, "Look at me, look at my friends, look at my interests. What friends do we have in common? If you like me, why don't we get in touch?"

- In direct selling, members are essentially saying, "Hey, I got this product that is really great. So let's talk and see if you want to buy it from me. If you do, I'll give you a good price and then you can get your friends and associates to buy it."

The authors of *The Social Media Bible*, Lon Safko and David K. Brake, pointed out that Facebook.com has more than 100 million registered users. "These social networks develop a trust that ultimately creates influence among your consumers. By developing and cultivating networks, your organization can create an opportunity to develop the trust that may result in sales."

13
Why Direct Selling Works

Direct selling capitalizes on the fact that you and I are social animals. We like to be with one another, work together, build together, create families and form communities. As social creatures, we need to band together, talk, exchange ideas and tell stories. Stories are how we learn and pass information from generation to generation. Storytelling is internally wired in us.

It only takes a very small investment to get into direct selling and from the start, you already have a system, organization and people that are in place.

After a brief orientation, you can start immediately earning money. From the outset, networking gives you a firm foundation on which to build, and once you enlist an army of people to work for you, you can cash in on geometric profits of leveraging.

QUICK STEPS: *BE REALISTIC.*

This is a description of how direct selling works. But, in reality, it takes varying amounts of time to earn enough income to support yourself.

Jimmy is the textbook case of what happens when network marketing works.

He put up $500 to get into Isagenix®. Seven and a half years later he had earned $20 millions dollars net and his business was generating $5 million dollars annually.

But, also remember, Jimmy paid his dues by learning network marketing before he hit it big betting on Isagenix®. Jimmy helped Isagenix® and Isagenix®, with its top management and product line, helped Jimmy. Sharing and cooperation worked like a dream for Jimmy and many others in Isagenix®.

What appealed to Jimmy about network marketing is that the risks are much less in terms of your initial investment—far less than those for a start-up business or a franchise. In successful network marketing companies, the heavy lifting has been done. The products, organization and structure have been tested and refined.

If your talents lie in organizing and managing people, direct selling is ideal for you. Once you get your basic team up and running, you can watch it and your profits grow.

People think that you have to get into direct selling as soon as a new direct selling company starts up. They want to be in on "a ground-floor opportunity" and at the top of the pyramid. Unfortunately, 99% of direct selling companies fail within 12 to 24 months. So most people will lose their investments plus all that time and energy. That is why your level of risk in direct selling relies heavily on the direct selling company you choose.

Jimmy Says: "The company must be past the risk stage and well into growth and momentum stage. Once a company reaches $3 to $4 million in monthly sales, it will reach a point of critical mass, where people around the company begin to hear of its success and will be strongly compelled to participate. This will start the super-exciting phase of explosive growth!"

In contrast to most network marketing companies that fail or stagnate, a company like Isagenix® has dynamic sales and momentum. If you get involved now, you may not be as successful as Jimmy, but if you work hard, you certainly should do well. I'm convinced that your risk-reward with Isagenix® is better than investing in most other types of businesses and specifically, in network marketing.

Isagenix® is hardly the only success story, though. The successful network-marketing companies are structured to leverage sales and income and produce high rates of return on their investments. Just look at the success of Amway, Avon, Mary Kay and NuSkin. Although all of these companies have been around for a while, in 2009, Amway made $8 billion in 2009, Avon $3 billion and NuSkin did $1.2 billion. Many other network-marketing companies earned hundreds of millions of dollars.

Learn from Direct Selling Failures

You can learn a lot about direct selling companies by studying why some of them fail. This happens for a number of reasons: they don't have the right product, the right systems or the right payment plan.

However, the main reason for failure is that they are more focused on making money than they are on offering valuable goods and services. These companies are impatient; they don't want to do all the hard work of developing a great product that customers will love. Instead, they want to make an immediate score and never build customer loyalty.

Successful direct selling companies have a high ratio of customers to distributors. Their products are in demand, deliver real value for the money and they sell well. Poor companies have low customer to distributor ratios; they are essentially selling their compensation plan , their get-rich-quick scheme, not their goods. They make their money by adding distributors, not from product sales. However, sooner or later, their flow of new recruits will stop and their businesses will collapse. Poor direct selling companies are what gives direct selling its negative reputation. Poor companies rely upon the greater fool theory where you keep selling a bunch of numbers that are not tied to any valuable products. The numbers cannot be sustained because there are few real customers. Again money, not value, is being exchanged.

> **QUICK STEPS:** *YOU CAN HELP YOURSELF.*
>
> Find out the direct selling company's ratio of customers to distributors. 81% of those who buy from Isagenix® each month are simply product users. Many companies have half that or less. Beware.

Direct selling even helps your personal development. It teaches you leadership and how to deal with and get the most from people. The education you receive from your upline (your sponsors) is invaluable, representing an enormous return on your investment in direct selling. Just as a person example, Jimmy spent hours with me explaining the ins and outs of the business. You too will find that your mentors can tell you all sorts of ways that you can succeed in the business. After all, it's to their advantage.

That's not to mention the social aspect. Often, we fail to recognize in this fast-paced world how lonely people are. Direct selling brings people together and gives them connection to other human beings.

In direct selling, you get on the phone, you talk to people, you go out and have meetings. You can talk to your sponsors. They can be your therapist, your mentor, trainer or friend. You get support from many quarters because people in the company's office are frequently in touch with you.

Direct Selling's Advantages

Here's a summary of some of the advantages of direct selling I covered and some additional benefits:

1. *Investment.* You only have to make a small initial investment. Often it's only a few hundred dollars.

2. *Mini franchise.* It's a copy-cat system. You learn how to succeed in business in general, and specifically in direct selling. Once you are taught the system by your direct selling company and your sponsors, you can teach it to other people.

3. Education. Good MLM companies give you the free tools and resources to educate yourself on the products so that you can then educate others.

4. *Leverage.* When you recruit distributors, it increases your productivity and the rate of return on your investment of time and money because you can maximize your resources and effort through the efforts of others.

5. *Compounding.* The money you make continues to pour in whether you work or not because your downline keeps working for you. This is the definition of an asset—it puts money in your pocket whether you work for it or not. If your downline keeps growing, you are making money on your distributors and your distributors' distributors, and their distributors. This has a compounding effect as more and more distributors keep adding to your stream of money. Remember, 400 plus people join Jimmy's downline each day, and he gets a cut of any revenue they generate!

6. *Product use benefit.* You get to enjoy the use of the goods and services yourself. If you deal in items you like, you can buy them at a discounted price.

7. *Social.* Direct selling is a people business. You will meet interesting people and have continual contact with others with whom you can build relationships, form liaisons, compare notes and learn from each other. You also get a family and support and a buffer against loneliness and hard times that we all face from time to time.

8. *Flexible hours.* Since you operate your own business, you can set your own hours and determine when and how much you work.

9. *Low entry barrier.* You don't need a college degree, any particular experience, licenses or certifications to get in the direct selling business. All you need is a little start-up money and the desire.

10. *Team work.* You get to be a member of two teams: your upline team and your downline team. With your upline, you join, learn from and

interact with an established team. You also get to build, shape and teach your downline team.

11. *Global reach.* By using the Internet, you can reach people all over the world. You can recruit them for your downline or as your customers.

12. *Growth.* If you recruit the right people, they will also recruit good people so your downline and your business will grow.

13. *Additional resources are available on a temporary basis.* When you need particular resources, you can hire them as independent contractors. For examples, a bookkeeper, a computer technician or attorney. You can hire them only for the time you need them to keep your costs down.

14. *Product innovation.* The network-marketing company pays for expensive product and service innovation. Good network-marketing companies are always trying to develop new outstanding items.

15. *Product delivery.* Network-marketing companies provide product ordering and delivery systems as well as customer service, which frees you to concentrate in other areas.

16. *Technology.* Network-marketing companies develop and provide you with the latest technology. They provide your website, your customer/distributor sign-up and ordering systems, your order tracking and delivery systems and your commission calculation and payment systems. They also furnish training programs and materials in a number of formats including audio, video and text.

17. *Home based.* Your business can be run from your home so you don't have to commute. You can deduct your home office from your taxes and can enjoy spending more time at home.

18. *Personal change.* Direct selling can be ideal for people who are disabled, have lost their jobs or want to change their lifestyles and/ or careers.

Can you take advantage of these network-marketing benefits and become a network-marketing success story yourself?

Here is an excellent article from ArticlesBase.com that confirms some of the key points I have emphasized so far:

"Many networkers look at the success stories of MLM and want to be able to emulate them. The good news is that these successes are just regular people who learned skills that you can learn to.

The simple truth is that there is a large gap between people who want success but do not take the necessary steps and those who attain it. In other words, there are a lot of "wannabe's" in the business who never make it.

So, what do the success stories of MLM do in order to be the winners they are?

1. **Daily Habits.** Successful network marketers are actively working on their business every day. How they do this, is different for everyone. Some may simply set a goal of two new prospects a day, perhaps by adding to new people to an opt-in mail list, face to face contact with two people who are interested in their story, adding new friends to social networking friend's list (e.g. on Facebook) or giving away free information such as a report, newsletter, or e-book download.

2. **Weekly Habits.** The highest earning network marketers also act consistently to build their business on a weekly basis with scheduled weekly activities...For example, some may choose to mail out one package a week to someone who they think would gain from hearing about their product or MLM opportunity. This can include a CD, free sample, pamphlets, or a book. This is a very effective way to let someone know you are in business without heavy selling.

3. **Monthly Habits.** No matter what business you are in, to be successful you have to keep up to date and keep learning. MLM is no different. Leaders who succeed attend the monthly events sponsored by their organizations. These events are usually enjoyable

and include dinners, lunches, seminars etc. They are designed to improve knowledge and prospecting skills as well as to encourage and motivate.

4. **Self Improvement.** The people who succeed in MLM are those who working to improve themselves. They take advantage of personal development resources such as books, Audios, DVDS, and participating in online groups etc. They tend to spend at least fifteen to thirty minutes every day on personal development.

5. **Don't Quit.** People who succeed in MLM know that success doesn't happen overnight. In fact, you may not see much happening for one, two or even three months. Successful network marketers know that MLM systems are designed to create exponential growth and the start up is always slow. They are fully aware that they have to be prepared to invest at least one year in building a new MLM business and they are committed to the process. They don't get distracted by every new opportunity that comes along.

6. **Create an "Edge."** The most successful people in MLM are focused on maintaining a slight edge. They are well aware that it is easy to avoid taking the necessary actions for success. But they are also aware that those actions are equally easy to do if they are disciplined to do them. They choose to take personal responsibility for their success or failures in life and in business. Even if they can't see any immediate benefits from their daily actions, they are committed to doing them anyway because they know there will be long term benefits. The biggest MLM producers know that while 80% of their time may need to be invested in building their business, in the long run this will reduce to 20% of their effort and they will reap the benefits.

7. **Have a Long Term View.** Finally, the success stories of MLM are able to live outside their "comfort zone" for a period of time because they are aware that they will reap huge benefits in usually three to five years.

It is clear that people who succeed in MLM have a different approach to individual's who remain simply "wannabe's." If you genuinely want to succeed in MLM, you can choose to follow the example of those who have succeeded and put yourself on the pathway to success."

(Source: "Become a MLM Success Story" by Kevin Sinclair)

The Instant Gratification Trap

In the Performance Economy, speed is the new drug. Everyone wants everything immediately; they insist of instant gratification and hate to wait.

People live at breakneck speed; everything is done in a blur. The line between business and our personal lives has virtually disappeared. No longer do we have separate hours for each of them. Now we're constantly on our cell phones—when we drive, in waiting rooms and restaurants—no place is cell phone free. We don't care who it disturbs. We wake up to check emails, and we welcome interruptions because it may be an important business matter.

When technology brought us instant communications and 24/7 access, it also gave us a heightened sense of urgency. It increased our impatience and created unrealistic expectations and views of the world.

People felt entitled to receive everything now. They didn't want to build, grow or develop—they wanted it all now.

- Instant gratification destroys wealth—monetary and non-monetary.
- Deferred gratification creates long-term success in business and in life.

In the late 1960s a test was conducted at Stanford University by researcher Walter Mischel, to measure four-year-olds' self-control and ability to delay gratification. The researchers gave the children the choice of eating a marshmallow right away or waiting. Those children who were willing to wait (up to 20 minutes) while the researcher stepped out of the room would be given two marshmallows when the researcher returned. A bell was placed at each child's desk that the child could ring if he or she wanted the researcher to return to the room. When the researcher returned, the child was allowed to eat one marshmallow, but not the second.

Most of the children ate their marshmallow within three minutes. About 30% held off until the researcher came back, which was about 15 minutes on average.

When the study followed the children into young adulthood, it found that:

- Children who held out the least appeared to have behavioral problems both at home and in school. They had difficulty handling stress circumstances, paying attention and maintaining friendships.

- Children who waited only 30 seconds also scored lower on S.A.T. tests. They averaged 210 points lower those children who successfully delayed gratification for 15 minutes.

Direct selling is not a shortcut to wealth, but it can be a fabulous way to get rich. You have to be patient and understand that it will take time to put all the pieces in place. Some people make lots of money immediately, but for most it takes time. Direct selling is no different than any other business: it must be built. And that usually doesn't happen overnight.

If you go into direct selling, learn the ropes and build your base— your downline which you can leverage into more and more customers and distributors.

Forget instant gratification if you want to be in the top 1% of successes.

Jimmy Smith notes, "For 14 years prior to Isagenix®, I had saturated myself. I was totally engulfed in network marketing, so everything I did for 14 years prepared me for Isagenix®. When I joined Isagenix®, all systems said go. I was ready."

Have you heard about the *Ten Year Rule*? The books *Talent is Overrated* by Geoff Colvin and Malcolm Gladwell's *Outliers* point out that child prodigies who became outstanding achievers went through a preparatory period for at least 10 years.

This incubation period is called "deliberate practice." Deliberate practice was conducted by teachers including Mozart's and Tiger Woods' fathers. During the deliberate practice period, people hone their skills. They learn, practice, and go through trial and error until they master their craft.

You can't do it all yourself. Many factors contribute to success. It takes a lot of practice to be the best. It also takes education and teaching from the best. Direct selling by its design provides the experience and teaching of the network marketing company itself—their winning formula such as Isagenix®, Amway, Mona Vie, Mary Kay, Avon

Most people won't make that investment. They're too impatient. Don't make the same mistake.

QUICK STEPS: *INVEST IN YOURSELF.*

Invest in Your Destiny. Don't look for the quick hit. Be patient, take your time, build, learn and after you do, it will all fall in place.

14

Is Direct Selling for You?

All businesses have drawbacks and are not right for everyone. Direct selling is no exception. Certain people will not do well in direct selling and others won't like it. So, before you take a stab at direct selling, take a few moments to consider whether the business is likely to be a good fit for you.

Do you have the right qualities to be a great network marketer? The major requirement is that you work well with others because direct selling is a people business that requires constant personal interaction.

To succeed in direct selling, you must get along well with others and be able to work well with them. Answer the following questions to see if the direct selling business is right for you:

- *Are you a loner?* Certain people just want to be alone. You may not be comfortable interacting with others. You may be shy or overly sensitive to others' criticism. You don't do well in groups, although you may be fine by yourself. Typically, you should avoid direct selling.

- *Do you like interacting with others?* Are you a people person who enjoys collaborating, leading and working with others? Do you have good social and interpersonal skills? If so, direct selling and social networks could be right up your alley.

- *Are you comfortable setting up your own mini-business?* Are you enterprising? Would you like to set up your own business and motivate others with their mini-businesses? If you like challenges, building relationships and making things grow, direct selling could be ideal for you. It also helps if you like to strategize, plan and manage.

There are time considerations as well. How much time must you devote to your direct selling business and still have a life? In the beginning, when you first become involved with direct selling, it can be very time-consuming and you may not have time for much else. Starting up or going into any new business can eat up much of your time. If you can't or don't want to put in that time, direct selling probably isn't for you.

You should also ask yourself how important it is to you to become rich. Is it worth sacrificing other parts of your life? Everything we do has a price, and the price to succeed in business, any business, is often steep. To succeed in direct selling you must be devoted and put in lots of effort and time. If you have a family and other obligations, they may have to take a back seat—at least in the beginning. However, many family members end up going into direct selling together as a way to have more time with one another.

When you are established in direct selling, you will be better able to balance your time. You'll know the system, the time and effort required, have better contacts and have learned shortcuts. You will also be able to work smarter, more efficiently and have learned when and to whom to delegate.

Jimmy estimates that you have to put in at least three or four hours every day. That means you could keep your job and still do this. **Jimmy says:** "I remember when my daughter Kathy started. She had seven children, and she worked at a daycare taking care of ten children, so that was 17. When she got all her chores done at the end of the day, she'd drive a half hour to my office, which is about 50 miles away. She'd stay with me all evening until 12 o'clock at night because she wanted it. She really wanted it bad. Now she's making millions of dollars every year."

Those are the major considerations, but let me offer some more for you to think about. Answer honestly. They are:

1. Do you love to lead people?

2. Do you enjoy teaching and seeing your students succeed?

3. Are you a follower?

4. Are you coachable?

5. Are you generous and willing to share or do you want all the credit?

6. Do you think that people will follow you?

7. Do you believe that you can be successful?

8. How badly do you want it?

15

Comparisons With Direct Selling

"Patience and perseverance have a magical effect before which difficulties disappear, and obstacles vanish."

— John Quincy Adams

Traditionally, the primary advantages of holding a job, as opposed to running your own business, were:

1. Your job provided you with a steady income.

2. You had job security.

3. You got health, pension, retirement and other benefits, depending on your employer.

Now it's all changed. The reality is that jobs are no longer secure. Employees can lose their jobs at any time for virtually any reason, even the best of them. Today, you can be in the corner suite and tomorrow, you can be out on the street.

Getting a job is harder. Currently, jobs are in short supply as companies wait to see if the economy will turn. Most are still reeling from the affects of the recent Great Recession when real unemployment figures soared into the mid-to-upper teens.

Even if employees have job security, which is increasingly rare, their income isn't likely to grow a lot unless they're top performers. As employers have been financially squeezed, they have cut back across the board, including on wages, pay raises, bonuses and sales commissions.

Despite all the problems, many people are delighted just to have a job. Having a steady job has its advantages, but one of them is not getting wealthy. With a job, your time is not your own; you do not have personal freedom. There are trade-offs that only you can evaluate.

When compared to the jobholders, the major disadvantages of direct selling are:

1. You must make an initial investment.

2. You don't have a steady income.

3. It could take you three to five years to make more than you could as an employee.

4. Only 10% of network marketers exceed what they earned when they were employed.

In comparison to jobholders, the major advantages of being a network marketer are:

1. You're your own boss—you call the shots.

2. You set your hours—personal freedom.

3. Your earning power is unlimited—chance for financial independence.

Here are some other differences between having a regular job and being a network-marketing distributor. They are:

Holding A Regular Job	**Being a Network Marketer**
Income stops if you:	*Income continues if you:*
a. Are fired	a. Work or not
b. Quit	b. Quit
c. Become disabled	c. Or become disabled
Your time is not yours if:	*Your time is yours if:*
a. You work for someone else	a. You work for yourself
Income limits	*No income limits*
a. By hour worked	a. Not limited by hours worked
Lack of leverage	*Leverage*
a. Trade time for dollars	a. Paid for both time and other people's time
Linear growth pattern	*Geometric growth pattern*
a. 1, 2, 3, 4, 5, 6…	a. 1, 2, 4, 8, 16, 32…
b. Does not compound	b. Compounds
Wealth created	*Wealth created*
a. Typically, little	a. Potentially, a great deal

Franchise Versus Direct Selling

Your choices are not limited to whether you remain an employee or not. Clearly, many people who are looking to break out of the "employee trap" look to both direct selling and franchising as options. Let's look carefully at your choices as you want to evaluate carefully the pros and cons between franchising and direct selling. Both can be lucrative. Now, let's compare franchising with direct selling:

Franchising	Direct Selling
High start-up costs	Low start-up costs
Income—linear growth	Income—exponential growth
Few or many Employees	Few or no employees
Usually not home-based	Home-based
Hours—controlled by business	Hours—flexible
Location—territorially based	Location—no limitations
Pay monthly fees	Paid by company commission
Various types of advertising	Word of mouth advertising

Franchises require larger up-front cash investments—often tens to hundreds of thousands of dollars. However, with top franchises, you usually have greater certainty of quickly generating revenue and making a return on your investment.

Names and brands carry more weight with franchises. In direct selling, a company's name or brand does not guarantee sales. However, if you become a McDonald's or a Subway franchisee, your odds of success exceed those in direct selling.

Jimmy Smith's interest in network marketing started when he wanted to have a business. He researched franchises and didn't think they made too much sense. He would have to hire teenagers and invest a million dollars, which he didn't have.

Jimmy says: In 1990 network marketing earned $20 billion dollars. Last year it did $120 billion. By the year 2020, it will earn a trillion dollars. Network marketing, somewhere around 2020 to 2025, will replace franchising as the number one way to move goods and services to the end consumer. Network marketing right now is where franchising was 50 years ago. Just imagine, back then a bill came up in Congress. They wanted to ban franchising forever; they said it was a scam. Right now 30 percent of the goods and services sold in the free world are sold through franchises. Somewhere between 20 and 25 are sold through network marketing, the wave of the future. This paradigm shift is taking place right now. Because of computers, because of cell phones, because of Webinars—all the modern technology has played into network marketing.

There is another reason for that. The average person cannot afford a franchise today. Seven and a half years ago, I invested $500 in my Isagenix® business and powered that into $20 million dollars. There is no other place on the planet where you can do that.

Network marketing is here to stay, and all of those naysayers who have been calling it a pyramid for years and years and years can cry all the way to the bank. Recently someone said to me, "Jimmy, is that one of them pyramids?"

I said, "Michael, call it what you want. I call it sweet. You call it whatever you want, dude."

In the beginning, network marketing consisted mostly of household goods, soaps and liquids. Then skin care got very, very big. Today the fastest-growing companies are the ones that sell a product that is healthy: nutritional supplements. There is a reason for that. The wellness industry became popular because people are growing older; they are living longer. The fastest-growing percentage of our population right now is the group between 85 and 100. When you visit some of these beautiful people in nursing homes, they will say, "If I knew I was going to live this long, I would have taken better care of myself."

The wellness industry is going to reach a trillion dollars by the year 2020. In the next 10 years, economist Paul Zane Pilsner predicts that 10 million new millionaires will be made in the United States. A large percentage of them are going to come out of the wellness industry. That's because network marketing will be a trillion dollar industry in the next 10 years.

Driving that growth is e-commerce, or business done through the Internet, which is going to be a multi-trillion-dollar industry. The Internet is going to be the biggest selling tool in the history of mankind. We all know that. It is growing faster than anything ever before, because everybody has a computer. The world is getting smaller and smaller. If you are part of one of those growing trends—if you are in wellness, or network marketing, or e-commerce, you are in good shape. But think about being in all three at one time: you are in the wellness industry, selling through network marketing, and using e-commerce all together at one time. How cool is that?

Although network marketing requires a small up-front investment, it may take one to five years to make enough money to cover your business and personal expenses. In the meantime you have to supplement your income, borrow from someone or take the money out of your savings. The ongoing investment and carrying costs can mount up so that what appears to be a small initial investment in reality is much larger than you anticipated. This is a reason why so many people quit network marketing when they realize it takes a true commitment of time, money and resources like any other business.

If someone decides to do network marketing, I know beyond a shadow of a doubt if they commit and become passionate about their business, they can be financially independent. I don't know how long it's going to take them because I don't know how hard they're going to work or how seriously they're going to take it, but if they do what I did, they will be financially independent.

The only way you can fail in network marketing is to quit. I know that for a fact. That's what happens to most people. They think they're going to come in and get rich quick. It's not get-rich-quick. It's very simple, but it's not easy.

Adding to what Jimmy said, here's a major consideration when it comes to direct selling: essentially, direct selling is a sales business, and most people are not good at sales.

Most start-ups fail because of lack of sales. While network-marketing companies provide successful selling systems, on the average, distributors earn only 5% on their and their distributors' sales. So, you must sell a lot to make the numbers work.

16
Pyramid Schemes

This was the question that first came to my mind when my associate Hank asked me to get involved with the multi-level-marketing business and speak with Jimmy Smith. When I first spoke to Jimmy, I asked him flat out if Isagenix® was a pyramid scheme. Jimmy's answer surprised me. He said that Isagenix® is not a pyramid scheme, but that it is structured as a pyramid. **Jimmy says:** Absolutely. What do you know about pyramids? Tell me what you know about pyramids? There are pyramids in Egypt that have been standing for thousands and thousands of years. There must be something good about a pyramid if it can stand the test of time.

If you were to invert that pyramid, put it upside down, it wouldn't last. It would tumble over, wouldn't it? It couldn't stand on the point, could it?

Every business, every government takes the form of a pyramid. At the top is the chairman of the board, and under that person is the president, vice presidents, upper management, lower managements. If you work for a car company, for instance, down below you have guys making the cars and selling the cars. They're at the bottom of the pyramid. Most people work for 40 years at the bottom of the pyramid. You go up a couple rungs, but you're nowhere near the top, and you will never get to the top if you are there a hundred years.

The pyramid in network marketing is the same as any other business. A scheme is a good thing; a scam is a bad thing. There are pyramid scams, and they're bad. Pyramid schemes are good. Amway, Shaklee, Mary Kay, NuSkin, Herbalife, all of these multi-level marketing outfits are great companies. Amway did eight billion last year, Avon did three billion, NuSkin did 1.2 billion.

There are a hundred companies doing over a hundred million dollars in network marketing, and a few are doing over a billion so if it were illegal, they'd all go to jail. They'd all be in jail—because pyramid scams are illegal.

When someone makes a statement about network marketing like, "Only the people at the top make the money, if you don't get in early, you don't make money. People want you to buy products so they can make money on you. You have to bother your neighbors forever." All of that's a myth.

The federal government charged Amway, the granddaddy of all multi-level marketing companies, with being a pyramid scheme in 1975. Amway fought the case for four years, and their defense cost them millions of dollars. Yet they proved without a shadow of a doubt that network marketing is legitimate. It's not only a viable way for people to make a living, it's a legitimate way to move goods and services to the end consumer.

You have to understand what network marketing is and what it isn't. When an industry is making billions of dollars every year, that's called capitalism. In 2009, multi-level marketing made 120 billion. It's grown at the rate of 10% a year. By 2020, it will do a trillion dollars and by 2025, network marketing will pass franchising as the best way to move goods and services to the end consumer.

Jimmy is absolutely correct. Most successful businesses are structured like pyramids, as is the military. Actually, virtually all businesses have pyramid structures. A manufacturing company sells its goods to regional distributors. The distributors sell those goods to a wholesaler in each state. The wholesaler in turn sells the products to retailers, who then sell the products to the public.

In corporations, decision making and compensation in corporations flows from top to bottom. The person at the top usually receives the most compensation and has the final say. As the pyramid spreads downward, individuals at each descending level have less pay and say. In fact, CEOs of large corporations are paid up to three hundred times more than their company's average employee receives!

By nature, people organize in hierarchies; even our thought patterns are often hierarchical. Take Google, for example. Google searches are hierarchical.

Although network-marketing companies have a pyramid structure, not all pyramid schemes are scams if they are legitimate businesses.

Let's take a look at the three main types of pyramid schemes which you want to avoid. Certain pyramid schemes are scams because no value is exchanged. Those who get in first—the people at the top—get money from those who come in later into the scheme. The three main types of pyramid schemes that are scams are the investment-based scheme (Ponzi/Bernard Madoff pyramid scheme), the product-based scheme and the non-investment or non-product scheme (often called a naked pyramid scheme).

Ponzi schemes: Investors are promised an abnormally high return on their investment. In most cases, older investors are paid with money received from new investors because sufficient income is not made to pay the older investors the promised rates of return. Everything works out well as long as the funds invested by new investors are enough to keep paying the older investors. If the amount of new investor money cannot cover the promised rate of return to the older investors, the scheme unravels and investors are no longer paid.

Product-based pyramid schemes: A product is marketed, but it has little value compared to the amount of money charged for it. The promoters' objective is not to sell customers items that have real value, but to impress on distributors how much money they can make quickly if they sell the overpriced or worthless products to other distributors, who in turn, try to bring in their distributors. In this scheme, the promoters and the distributors at the top of the pyramid make all the money and those at the bottom of the pyramid are stuck with tons of worthless products. As time passes, distributors can't recruit more distributors to purchase the overpriced goods.

Since most product-based pyramid schemes offer products that don't sell well or have slim profit margins, the only way that distributors can make money is by bring in more recruits. At some point, the market becomes saturated because too many distributors are trying to sell the inflated items.

Legitimate network-marketing companies focus on selling products to customers, not on recruiting distributors or salespeople on whose sales they will get overrides, commissions and/or bonuses.

Non-investment or non-product pyramid scheme. This scheme is often called a naked pyramid scheme because the only exchange between people in the organization is money, not an investment or a product. In a naked pyramid scheme, those at the top bring in recruits who pay them for the right to recruit other people who will pay them. In this scheme, the people at the top quickly get rich and those further down the line usually do not.

How do you evaluate whether a company is running a pyramid scheme or whether it is a legitimate company? Pyramid schemes that are scams differ with each usually having its own special twist. Most rely on high-pressure sales tactics; however, the nefarious Bernie Madoff had people banging down his door to do business with him. That said, these scams share a number of the common factors listed below.

To determine whether a company is operating a pyramid scheme that is a scam or offering a legitimate network marketing opportunity, consider the following facts about what scams look like:

1. *Scams frontload*: They charge high start-up fees to join. They also charge a nonrefundable membership fee, for start-up kits and costs for mandatory training.

2. *Recruiting versus selling to customers*: They focus on recruiting distributors more than they try to have their products sold to customers for a fair markup.

3. *Multiple markups*: Products are marked up from distributor to distributor. Commissions are added at five or more levels of distribution so the end product tends to be overpriced and have little value to the end user.

4. *Get-rich-quick scheme*: Emphasis is on how quickly you can get rich rather than on how you can build a business systematically.

5. *List of sales leads*: They market lists of sales leads that typically have little or no value. However, the lists give the impression that the company has a strong interest in the product and that many potential customers exist who are just waiting to be sold. In reality, these lists have little value and have often already been milked. Pyramid schemes that are scams use the lists as inducements to sign people up and get them to fork over steep upfront fees.

6. *High-pressure motivational events or sales tactics*: At these events, promoters appeal to people's greed by promising get-rich-quick schemes if potential recruits sign up then and there. Promoters use themselves as examples of how much money recruits can make.

7. *Ratio of customers to salespeople*: Network-marketing companies operating as scams take in more money by recruiting distributors than they get for selling their products to customers. Note: The more direct customers a company has, the greater the true market demand for the company's product.

Now we have covered all of the basic business knowledge you need in order to become a success. In Part II. we are going to take you down to ground level. You have decided you want to become a network marketer. What, practically, do you need to know to become one of those people in the 1% zone?

PART II

NUTS AND BOLTS

17
Evaluating Direct
Selling Companies

Now that you've made the decision to go into direct selling, you must find the right company. To accomplish this search, you must conduct research, find out which companies appeal to you and thoroughly check them out according to the criteria I will lay out.

First, start by examining the goods and services they provide.

Then look into each company thoroughly, in great depth. What is its reputation?

1. Visit its website and see how it presents itself.

2. See if you can obtain brochures and printed materials.

3. Find out its strong and weak points.

4. Try to visit the company headquarters and at least one of its offices.

5. Talk with the office staff. Gauge their attitudes, feelings, mood and morale. Do they seem happy working for that company, or are they grumpy and glum?

6. Ask about their feelings about the company and its products.

7. Ask if they use its items and if they excited about the company's future.

8. Speak with customers, vendors and distributors. Ask them what they like and dislike about the company and how well they think it's run. Get their feelings about the company's products, their quality and how well they work. Ask how they could be improved, how well they hold up and whether they're easy and inexpensive to repair.

When evaluating a company, you need to look at its core magnets—what attracts customers and distributors. Evaluate each company's item according to its:

Magnetism

Does the item create excitement and elicit emotional responses? Do customers really want to buy it and say, "I just have to have that dress, that sofa, that electronic device? I can't wait to buy it." Do they feel it's special or something they really want or need? Will it make customers' lives easier or better?

Don't underestimate the importance of a company's reputation and brand. Consumers prefer to buy brands they know and trust. They also prefer to do business with companies that have great reputations. A strong brand usually means high quality and reliability. When you think of Isagenix®, Johnson & Johnson and Mercedes Benz, you immediately have a positive reaction because you know that you can trust their products.

Consumability

Ideally, an item should be consumable, something that customers need to repeatedly replenish. When customers keep reordering, businesses have steady income flows. And their profits usually increase because the cost of making and refilling reorders is usually less than the costs of initial sales.

Vitamins, food supplements, beauty products and pet care products are excellent examples of goods that must repeatedly be replenished. The nice thing about consumables is that when customers like them, they frequently sign up to receive them automatically and at regular intervals. Automatic reordering provides an annuity income for suppliers and lowers their fulfillment costs.

QUICK STEPS: *AUTOMATIC SHIPPING.*

Auto-ship is the heart of the direct selling business. This is where the leverage is, since both your customers and the downline of your distributors are automatically re-ordering.

Distinctiveness

Customers remember and gravitate to distinctive items, those that have special qualities and stand out. They want to buy unique items to distinguish themselves and that shows that they have good taste. For example, people like to get into new trends early and buy "designer" goods as they believe that it gives them a certain status.

Distinctive items reflect people's personal styles and how they wish to project themselves. Distinctive styles top the charts in the Performance Economy. They get people press coverage and makes them household names. It's how singers on *American Idol* land record contracts and parts in Broadway shows.

Tradition

When I was in the food business, I learned that people make certain associations as a result of their upbringing. If I tell you to visualize a "cookie," you will probably picture it as round. And it follows that most people gravitate toward the more traditional round shape. Most folks like the familiar; familiar is comfortable and safe. That's why new innovations usually take hold slowly—people need time to adapt.

Value

Look at items according to their value to potential customers. Ask two primary questions: (1) Will customers find those items beneficial and (2) will they be willing to pay the amount charged? Make a cost-benefit analysis from the customers' points of view.

Better yet, do customers feel that they are getting a bargain? If customers believe that the price they pay is well worth it, or even *less* than they would be willing to pay, they usually will be happy and loyal. Everybody wants a good deal. So try to give it to them because it builds repeat business, referrals, recommendations and good will.

Timeliness

Items must be current, in demand now. Customers don't want yesterday's items unless they get them at a fabulous price—and even then most won't be happy with them for too long.

Look at the introduction of the Apple iPad. People waited in line to buy it even though they knew that it probably had new-product kinks. Many people will pay a premium to be on the cutting edge. They want to be at the head of the pack, but no one wants to bring up the rear.

Being timely is crucial with problem-solving goods and services because older items may arrive too late. You want your product or service to be in demand today. Selling future solutions is harder because most people only act when a problem is staring them in the face. Many are reluctant to spend today for tomorrow.

Stability

Some fads are big hits and sell extremely well, but they don't last. Sooner or later all fads fade and disappear. Look for solid items that will last, goods and services that will be needed tomorrow as much as they are needed now, items that won't be the victims of new trends and technology.

In addition to being solid and stable, look for items that can be improved, refined, adapted and applied to different uses. For example, although certain food supplements have been around for decades, they are constantly being improved and enhanced. Frequently, stickers on the packaging tell you what's new.

Finally, when you check out a company's goods or services, make sure that:

1. Its features are easily explained.

2. Its benefits are clear to customers and distributors.

3. You would use what you're trying to sell.

Find Out How Hard the Training Is

Find out how much training is needed to sell a company's goods or services and how difficult that training is.

People do not like to become involved with products that are too complicated for them. To succeed in direct selling you need to know everything about the items you sell. You must be an expert who knows about them in depth. You have to be able to answer any questions about your goods.

You also need to understand marketing and selling and what it means to be part of the company, where you and your distributors fit in. So find out precisely what training is necessary, what the company provides and what will be required of them. What studying will you be required to learn on your own?

Also ask what training will be conducted, where, when and by whom? Learn what materials will be provided and whether any cost is involved.

The more you understand about the goods and services you sell, the better you will be able to sell them. The more you can sell, the better the opportunity. If you find a business is hard to learn, chances are that learning it will also be difficult for the people in your downline. You have to teach them eventually.

QUICK STEPS: *TEST WHAT YOU SELL.*

Test your products by using them yourself. Take Isagenix®. You need to know your products and it takes time. An excellent way to learn is to use the product you sell. When you do, you get on-the-job training. And when you have hands-on experience, you can usually describe the product better, talk about it firsthand and honestly know what you're talking about. People pick up on that.

Test whatever you sell; use it yourself. Then your customers will feel your enthusiasm when you say, "Here is how this works and how it will help you." Tell them about your own experience, what it felt like, how it worked and how you liked the ingredients.

Brands

Go with good companies, companies that have great brands. A brand is a powerful selling point that gives you a huge competitive advantage. A great brand can clinch sales because it says that the company has a reputation for reliability, quality and trust.

A company's brand is more than just its logo, slogan and name. It has a consistency that runs through every facet of the company and is reinforced in its look, positioning, communication and how it does business. The top companies have crafted their stories, their histories of how they were founded and how they grew. All that information is embodied in their brands. It's also contained in their messages, communications, their training materials, brochures and their products and services. When consumers see great brands, all that information instantly comes to mind.

Branding experts estimate it takes $50 million to make a brand a household name. As companies like Mary Kay, Amway or Isagenix® grow, they pour money into their brand's story and messages. They plaster it on everything because they understand the power of its impact.

Today, brand is defined by relationships. Top brands have large lists of members and/or customers.

In the case of direct selling, companies rely upon their customer and distributor network. If a company consistently performs well, its brand typically will reflect this by constantly innovating and adding new features to keep their customers engaged. As a result, its items will sell and the company will continue to grow.

Brands can no longer survive by just throwing a lot of marketing dollars on the table and pushing their name in your face. Today's marketplace can instantly voice its opinion of the company and its products on Twitter and other online social platforms.

Companies like Dell and Comcast have learned that you must be responsive to your customers; treat them well and they will treat you well in return.

Packaging and Design

Most network-marketing companies don't put enough emphasis on packaging. Most products just go from manufacture to the end consumer/distributor. Network-marketing company products are not usually displayed in stores, so many companies don't put a lot of money or effort into packaging.

The problem is, people are visual. They buy with their eyes. You only have a fraction of a second to get their attention. If your product looks unappealing, they may decide it lacks quality and has less value. Look at Apple's products—the iPhone, iPod, iPad, actually the entire Apple product line. They all have an iconic look. People want Apple products because they look so great. Design sells.

Many companies make a huge mistake by not investing in their logo, looks and packaging. Design is growing in importance and it is now a major factor in buying decisions, especially for people with disposable income.

Evaluate the look and design of a company's items. How do they strike you? When you speak to people, how do they respond to the company's designs? Design is an indication of a company's planning. It reflects the direction of a company and its taste level. It also shows how the business wants to position itself and its items in the market.

Opportunity Checklist

Deciding which business to enter isn't easy. A lot will be on the line. To help with your decision, make two lists for each opportunity. First, list all the reasons why you should go with this opportunity and second, make another list of why you should not.

Many people are poorly matched with their jobs. So they end up hating their jobs. Make sure that direct selling is a good match for you. Otherwise, you probably won't succeed.

Before you make your final decision, answer the questions on the checklist below. It can help you make a better decision. The questions are:

- ❑ Is this an industry in which you wish to be involved?
- ❑ Is this a company with which you would wish to be involved?
- ❑ Does this company deal in a product or products with which you would wish to be involved?
- ❑ Is this a brand that you or your associates know and respect?
- ❑ What specific training will you receive now and in the future?
- ❑ When, where and how will your training take place and with whom?
- ❑ How is the management structured and how good is it?
- ❑ What is the compensation plan?
- ❑ How and when will you be compensated?
- ❑ Will you have sponsors and what will your relationship with him/ her be?

❏ How extensive is your downline and what will be your relationship with it be?

❏ Will you have an exclusive customer pool?

❏ If not, what customers can you and others pursue?

❏ If you have distributors, what will your relationship with them be?

❏ Can this opportunity realistically fulfill your goals?

❏ Is this a long-term opportunity or just for the short run?

❏ Are you passionate about this opportunity, this company and its goods or services?

❏ Will you be willing to focus on and devote yourself to this opportunity?

    ❏ Full time?

    ❏ If less than full time, how much?

❏ What three people do you know or can reach to consult about this opportunity?

All of these decisions are crucial to both your future success in direct selling and your happiness. If a product is not well made, you will get tired of making excuses to dissatisfied customers. If a product is too complicated for you to understand, how long do you think you'll keep saying, "I don't know the answer to that question"? If it's not well designed, nobody is going to want it in the first place. So be smart about your choice. Research the product and talk to people in the company. Those are the first steps in what could become a very happy relationship.

Take Your Family

In June 1984, Blake M. Roney, started Nu Skin with less than $5,000 start-up capital, which was from his own pocket. Twenty years later Nu Skin's sales exceeded $1 billion. Roney said, "When you become a successful distributor, people will want to become like you. Be the kind of person worthy of emulation. Most important, take your family with you. They should be the most important part of your life. Don't make the mistake of reaching the top without your family."

One of the secrets of success is to be a person others will want to emulate. **Business success is about leadership development.** The top producers become top leaders. They not only march up front and set the pace, they organize those who follow and they stimulate them, which motivates both their followers and themselves. Top leaders project a vision and inspire people to become irresistible forces so they can reach the vision and benefit from its accomplishment.

You also become a leader by showing people that you have a good personal life, Roney pointed out. Don't be a workaholic and leave your family behind. Instead, involve your family. Their support is critical to your overall success in life.

When Jimmy went to his first network marketing meeting, the company's representatives tried to convince him to join the firm. Jimmy rejected the opportunity because he didn't see any members of their family involved in the business and supporting them.

18

Company Management

You can buy the most beautiful car, a car that everyone would want to own, but you have to know how to drive it. You have to know how to get it safely from Point A to Point Z.

Businesses are the same. Everything can look great on paper, all the facts and figures. The product can be fabulous, the packaging beautiful and the sales force unparalleled.

But to succeed, all businesses must have strong and stable management. They must be financially sound, have vision and be well operated.

In direct selling, management's philosophy must be distributor friendly. Management must provide top-notch support for its distributors, including sales aids, promotional materials and most of all, a genuinely friendly, cooperative and appreciative attitude. They must employ top trainers who have successful track records.

Evaluating management can be tricky, especially for outsiders, because so many factors are involved and many of them are not easy to see. You have to dig, and that may not always be possible. While you may not be able to examine every detail, here are a number of items that you must evaluate.

Who's in Charge?

Find out who is running the company. What are their backgrounds, experience and track records? Where did they work before? What types of

131

goods or services did they work with? Find out how strong their commitment is to the company and its product line. Learn about their plans for now, the next year, five years from now and in a decade.

Don't blindly walk into an opportunity because a friend tells you how great it is. Word of mouth is fine to start, but then you have to check for yourself. Plus, how much does your friend truly know? Remember that you will be making a major investment, putting a lot on the line, so find out who is in charge and about his or her team.

When Jimmy investigated Isagenix®, he found the formulator of the product was John Anderson. Jimmy had heard of him and knew he had a good reputation.

John Anderson was known as the Mineral Man because he had championed minerals over the years, way before most people even knew the importance of minerals. John Anderson had come out of retirement to help start Isagenix®. He wanted to give products with no compromise. During his career, he had formulated and produced over 2,300 products for 600 different companies. He was a private labeler and would put their label on them. Many of those companies asked him to compromise on the ingredients, which he didn't want to do.

When he started Isagenix®, he guaranteed that he would not compromise on the ingredients. Whatever was supposed to be in the products, he guaranteed it would be there. If a product calls for 250 milligrams of selenium, Vitamin C or whatever, it's going to be there.

Jimmy also knew of Jim and Kathy Coover, the two other people starting the company. Jim had been in the network marketing industry for 25 years. He had been president and CEO of several companies that became very large. One company he was involved in back in the 1980s was the Cambridge Diet. That company, in 23 months, reached a billion dollars in sales, which is unprecedented in the multi-level marketing industry. His wife, Kathy, had been active in this industry as a distributor. She had risen to the top of the last three companies she was involved with. Jim would handle the corporate end and Kathy was in the field, so Jimmy knew that the company had a solid basis.

He was looking for another quality too. He found that Jim and Kathy Coover and John Anderson had integrity. They were down to earth, they were real people. There was no hype or phoniness; they just told it like it was. Seven and a half years later, he relates, they haven't changed a bit. They're the same people they were. All this money and success didn't go to their head. They're not egomaniacs. They brought on the right people. They knew they needed help if they were going to take this company to a billion dollars in sales.

They created one of the best management teams Jimmy has ever seen in any industry. He recognized that from day one. As he notes, "This industry teaches you to read people very well. I read them very well and felt very good about them. I wanted to be partners with them. They made me partner in their business for $39, which I thought was great. My original investment was $500 seven and a half years ago and that's turned into $20.5 million. It was a good investment."

You can do the same. Find out who's running the company. Find out what their commitment is to their product. I'll repeat: don't walk blindly into an opportunity because a friend tells you how great it is. Is she going to be left holding thousands of dollars worth of products when the company files for bankruptcy?

Again, Jimmy cautions, **"You are judged by the 'company' you keep. The corporate office must have leaders in their fields (i.e., scientists and other professionals, with known and proven records). In other words, they must be credible."**

Communication

Good management requires good, clear communication. Otherwise, too many mistakes can be made and important tasks may not be properly completed. Managers must clearly communicate. They must leave no doubt as to what must be done and when it needs to be accomplished. All work must be constantly monitored to assure that it proceeds on schedule.

Ask about the order of command and the lines of communication. Find out who is in charge of what. Specifically ask how directives and information will be given to you. Look for direct lines of communications that don't go through a number of intermediaries.

Also try to find out if you will be given freedom to do your work or whether you will be micromanaged.

Some companies have strict rules and procedures that can't be changed. They insist on tasks being performed in certain specific ways. Others are more flexible as long as their people produce.

Is Innovation Part of Their Culture?

You've already investigated the company's goods and services, so now find out where it's heading. Learn about the company's efforts to keep improving its items, its management and other segments of its operation. What concrete plans has it made and what is on the drawing board?

Look for a company that is focused on always moving forward. See if it has been going backward or compromising. Does a company-wide commitment exist to continually keep trying to improve every aspect of the operation?

Remember, management guru Peter Drucker said that business is fundamentally about innovation and marketing. People like novelty. They want to know what's new. Jimmy Smith was attracted to Isagenix® because its co-founder John Anderson had a proven track record in health product formulas of superior quality for numerous top companies.

Check Out Their Website

How strong is the company's website and how great is its web presence?

Does it have a terrific-looking website that's filled with valuable and helpful information?

Is the site clear, easy to read and navigate, and does everything work?

Discover how many people visit the company website, how much business the company does because of it and its plans to improve, upgrade or change their site.

Try to evaluate the website and then discuss your likes and dislikes with company personnel. Check their reactions. See if they listen to your comments and are open to your suggestions.

A website gives you clues about the network-marketing company you are evaluating. Great websites take time and money to design and to make it easy for visitors to navigate. Websites act as giant business cards. They reflect a company's commitment to the Web and its positioning to the world. The Web is becoming more and more important to direct selling. Does the company give you the impression that they are seeking to be a cutting-edge company?

Your Upline

Get the names of the people in your upline and whether they will be giving you support. If they will, find out what that support will be.

In direct selling, your sponsor—the person who brings you into the company—and your upline can be the key to your success. If he or she is a leader, it can open doors for you, teach you shortcuts and how you can get ahead. Those in your upline can give you information about other people in the company and what you should do to get the most from them.

When you have a strong upline, it will help you build a great downline. It will teach you exactly what to do and what to avoid. It will also show you how to lead others and maximize their productivity.

Use people in your upline for three-way conference calls. If you're just starting out but you know a lot of people, your sponsor will say to you, "Make a list of at least 200 names, emails, phone numbers. If you don't make a list of 200 people, you're telling your sponsor that you're not serious. If you come back with 25 people and say, "This is all I know," your sponsor is going to answer, "Come on, more than 25 people. Go back to work; get that list up to 200."

That's because your 200 names become your sponsor's warm market by his association with you. You know 200 people he doesn't know. Then you give those 200 people a call and tell them what you're doing, and ask them if they would be willing to get on the phone with your sponsor. That's your up-line, your sponsor, your coach.

Your warm market becomes his warm market. Doesn't it behoove your sponsor to work with you to try and find some good people out of your list? His success depends on your success. That's the strongest tool in this industry, holding three-way calls. If you get your prospects on the phone with your sponsor, your sales are going to go way up.

The system works by simple human nature. If you don't succeed, your sponsor doesn't succeed. You have a vested interest in each other. That process goes all the way down.

QUICK STEPS: *HOW TO SELECT THE*
BEST NETWORK MARKETING COMPANIES.

Darren C. Falter, in his book *How to Select a Network Marketing Company: Six Keys to Scrutinizing, Comparing, and Selecting a Million-dollar Home-based Business,* gives the following criteria for selecting the best company. They are:

1. *Profit.* If money is your goal, as it is for most people, choose a company that will enable you to make a lot of money.

2. *Industry.* Find an industry in which you wish to work. Jimmy surveyed his options and decided that he wanted to go with a company in the nutritional supplement and personal care businesses. Make sure that you feel good about anything you may have to sell.

3. *Timing.* Get in at the right time, not after the trend has passed. Get in early, when the company is established and on the upswing. If you get in too early, you can get hurt because many companies haven't worked out the kinks and some never will. If you come in too late, the market may be saturated.

Does It Sound Too Good to Be True?

Little of real value is free. Virtually everything comes at some cost. When something sounds too good to be true, it usually is.

In business, the term "doing due diligence" means carefully checking things out before you get involved. Check out if what the direct selling company offers is truthful and all the numbers add up.

No one other than Oprah Winfrey and Ellen DeGeneres gives money away—regardless of what they may say. When you get any offer, or any proposition, always ask yourself, does this sound too good to be true?

Companies will woo you. They will flatter you and make promises to get you on their team. In direct selling, that's their business—to sign you up, to get you to join their company. If they think that you have potential, they may promise you the moon. Watch out!

If you're offered far greater returns than are available in the marketplace, ask why they are being offered to you. Chances are, there's a catch. It takes good luck to beat the average returns and good luck generally runs out.

Some companies are truly wonderful; others are bogus and only pretend to be. Some have great integrity, others do not. In any business, frauds, schemers and charlatans are always lurking to rip you off, and direct selling isn't immune. It's just like any other business, but fortunately, many network-marketing companies are legit.

QUICK STEPS: *DO YOUR DUE DILIGENCE*
OR WHAT I CALL DISCOVERY.

How?
Be cautious.
Do your homework, your due diligence.
Look before you leap.
Carefully analyze all offers and run them by people you trust.
Take the time to position yourself with the right company, the right industry, the right products and the right payment plan.

When evaluating a direct selling company, look under the hood. Be a mechanic. You may not find this part of the process glamorous. It's much easier to fall for all the hype and the adulation because you are a target. Every network-marketing company wants another recruit. That's their business to sell you on them.

It's your business to do the best for you. That means you have to get into the nuts and bolts—the nitty-gritty, whether you are a grease monkey or not. At first, you may feel uncomfortable asking the hard questions that I am laying out for you, but they won't be as hard as answering the questions your unhappy customers will be asking you later.

In the end, it comes down to:

1. What are the real numbers that the company itself is earning?

2. How many customers do they have versus distributors?

3. How long have has the company been in business?

4. What is the experience of management?

5. Does the company overemphasize the payment or compensation plan?

Here's what I'd like you to do. Project out into the future, whether you are new to direct selling or not. Once the big rush and the big projections are in the drawer, is this what you want to commit your life to? If your answer is yes, this means you will become a distributor. Let's look at what that means for you and your path to potential riches in direct selling.

19

What It Means to Be a Distributor

As a network-marketing distributor, you have an unusual status. You are sort of a hybrid in terms of your rights, duties and where you stand. The following is a brief overview of what the job entails. Of course, exceptions and special situations always exist, but the following outlines how being a distributor usually works.

Your Ownership and Work Status

As a distributor, you don't own the direct selling company or any part of it. The company does not give you health care or other benefits. You have to buy those yourself. It doesn't supply an office and you pay all your own expenses.

Distributors are not the direct selling company's employees. They are independent contractors, which means that you work for yourself. When you are paid, sums are not withheld for taxes. It's the distributor's—your— responsibility to pay them.

To be a distributor, you must become a member of the network-marketing company. That means that you have to adhere to the company's rules and requirements. In most cases, you join to get a business in a box, a system with tested procedures that you follow in order to earn money. The company will allow you to use its system in order for you to market its goods or services. You can buy the company's items for yourself or sell them to your customers or other distributors.

What You Get

As a distributor, you earn a commission on your sales of the company's goods and services. You also get a percentage of the sales made by the people in your downline, those you recruited into your business network. The amounts you receive—your commissions—are paid according to the company's commission schedule. You also will be educated about business and personal growth based upon the company's materials, culture and your upline sponsors. It's like joining a loosely knit fraternity or sorority that has its own story, rules and ways of doing things except you get paid by your network rather than just being a brother or sister.

Some benefits to being a distributor:

- Most direct selling companies will give you discounts when you buy their products. Then you can either use the products for your personal benefit or mark up the products' prices and sell them to your customers for a profit. Or, you can sell products to distributors and get paid a commission on your sales to them and in turn be paid an override commission on their sales to other customers and distributors. This creates a stream of income from your initial sales efforts, and you piggyback on the sales efforts of those you recruit and the efforts of your recruits' recruits and so on for many levels dictated by your direct selling company's type of payment plan. This is positive leverage at its finest. Go get my free special report called "Mastering the Art of Leverage." Here's the link: **http://www.masteringtheartof leverage.com/** or **www.StepsTo.com**

- Most direct selling distributors oversee their downline from their home offices.

  This differs from the traditional distributors whose trucks you see speeding on highways across the U.S. Many of these major distributors, not networking-marketing distributors, have trucks, trains and even planes (FedEx). They are middlemen who buy goods in bulk at below wholesale, warehouse them and sell them at wholesale prices to retailers who sell them to you at retail, e.g., supermarkets. Frequently, these intermediaries are more like truckers than salespeople.

- Network-marketing distributors are more like salespeople. They usually don't store and deliver goods; the direct selling company does that for them.

- Instead, network-marketing distributors concentrate on recruiting people for their downlines, supervising their downlines and selling the company's goods or services.

QUICK STEPS: *YOU'RE REALLY A SALESPERSON.*

You may be called a distributor, but in reality you are a salesperson and you are paid as a salesperson a commission.

Why?

Companies such as Isagenix® do most of the work for you. They're highly mechanized and their systems run like clockwork. You put in the order, they fill it, ship it, bill for it and handle all of the accounting and paperwork. Their automatic reordering systems contact customers to reorder and then fulfill those reorders.

Since network-marketing companies like Isagenix® do the majority of the work related to the creation, marketing, movement and delivery of the goods, you are paid more for your sales efforts—a smaller amount compared to a traditional distributor with a truck. Technically, you are a distributor because you buy goods at one price and resell them. But your effective profit is much lower than a traditional distributor. When you calculate what you are being paid, it amounts to a sales commission. If you sell a lot, you get bonuses, which amount to higher sales commissions.

Direct selling companies make it easy. They do so much of the work that that their distributors can concentrate on taking orders and signing up more distributors—both are mainly selling functions.

How Do You Get Prospects to Join Your Downline?

If you want people to join your network as your distributors, you must tell your prospects about your experience with the company and outline the direct selling company's compensation plan.

When you give numbers, state how much you made and what they can earn.

You will find some people get excited—even before they try the product—and most want to learn more.

Be straight and honest with all prospects because you may be working with them if they join your network and become part of your downline. Create a feeling of trust from the very beginning.

When you're interested in a prospect, take a systematic approach similar to the AIDA formula:

A. Get the prospect's attention.

I.   Create interest by asking the prospect to review the materials.

D. Evoke the prospect's desire and

A. Act to get the prospect to join the network as a distributor.

Jimmy's sales success rests upon relationships first. Build trust and then sell. Most people do the opposite—and fail.

This is the same strategy used in social networking. To create a relationship and build trust, you must demonstrate that you are competent and reliable. On the Web, people blog and give their personal opinions without thinking about selling anything.

There's the story of blogger Robert Scoble who blogged about his employer Microsoft's product. What Scoble said was that Microsoft's

Internet browser was inferior to its young competitor's called Firefox. He was accurate. Many knew this in the community who had tried both. But no one believed he would have the courage to come out and say it.

Microsoft did not fire him. Soon people—tech geeks, business people and Microsoft loyalists—began following Scoble's blog.

Do you think people would buy a product that Scoble recommended?

Of course. Yet he did not have to sell.

Why?

Because people wanted to buy; they trusted him. He was not on the Microsoft's side. He was on the side of truth.

In Austin, where I live, the waiters and waitresses will tell you what's good and what is lousy on the menu. They are very accurate. Do I want to order from them, come back to the restaurant and give them a big tip? Of course. And they did not sell me. I wanted to buy.

Social networking, direct selling and selling all rest upon building relationships and trust first; then the sales come without you having to sell.

The same is true with dealing with people as a distributor. This is a people business. You are in the middle of a chain, with people above you and people below you. Once you learn to build trust on both ends, you will become a success.

20

Find the Best Prospects

When you're looking to find distributors to build your downline, it's always risky. People aren't always who they initially seem to be. You can easily make the wrong choice. Regardless how hard you try, no matter the questions you ask, you always can make mistakes.

However, if you go about it systematically and pay careful attention, you can cut your risks.

Finding good, honest, motivated, competent people is at the heart of your business. And unfortunately, there are no guarantees when it comes to people. To help you with your challenge, I've put together the following checklist. Use it as a guide. It can increase your chances of finding superstars:

1. Always rely upon your gut instinct. What intuitively do you feel about this person?

2. Always check prospects thoroughly by:

   a. Getting at least three references

   b. Calling the references

   c. Listening to whether the reference is being genuine

3. Evaluate how long they stayed at their prior jobs. Do the reasons they gave for leaving sound fishy?

4. Have they tried to go out on their own?

  a. What happened?

  b. Why did they fail?

  c. What industry were they in?

  d. Were investors involved?

  e. Did they invest their own money along with their investors?

  f. Did they draw a salary and/or benefits?

  g. Do they appear to want to go back in business for themselves?

  h. What role did they play in the company?

5. Did they move?

  a. What motivated the move?

  b. Do they live alone?

  c. Have a pet?

  d. Do they belong to groups and organizations? How social do they seem.

6. Appearance: Check their:

  a. Personal grooming

  b. Quality and appropriateness of clothing

  c. Attention to detail

  d. Anything indicating that the person is too made up

  e. Age appropriateness

  f. Posture, presence, composure and confidence.

7. Attitude:

  a. Positive?

  b. Negative?

  c. Arrogant

  d. Hostile

  e. Brash

     f.   Depressed

     g. Overly giddy

     h. Anxious

     i.   Defensive

8. Open vs. Closed:

     a. Coachable?

     b. Eager to learn?

     c. Respect wisdom?

     d. Biased?

     e. Know-it-all?

9. Motivation:

     a. Reasons for wanting to be a network marketer

     b. Other factors: Desires personal freedom; recognition; likes to teach; lead; mostly, make money (you want this a lot)

10. Technical skill set:

     a. Computers

     b. Electronics

     c. Money and finances

11. Marketing/Sales Experience:

Go in-depth regarding:

     a. Their specific experience

     b. Facts/figures. How much they sold

     c. Their contacts, networks and social intelligence

Conduct Interviews

Start by meeting with each candidate personally to form an impression of him or her. Trust your instincts and comfort level with each prospect.

QUICK STEPS: *TO FIND SUPERSTAR NETWORK MARKETERS TO BUILD YOUR DOWNLINE, START WITH THE END IN MIND.*

Before you meet with prospects, make a list of what you would want in the ideal candidate. List every quality you would like—whether it's realistic or not. Then list all of the qualities that you don't want.

After you make each list, prioritize each to clarify those traits that are the most important to you.

When you meet with prospects, you won't always learn many important things through your questioning, so you have to be observant and "read" prospects to get a sense of them.

Try to get indications of their energy level, their integrity and attitude. Look for the following:

- Do they look you in the eye?
- If they shake your hand, how firm and confident is their grip?
- When they shake your hand, do they look away?
- Do you like their general demeanor or is their something about them that makes you feel a bit uneasy?
- Do they ask constructive questions, give you intelligent feedback and seem to have a genuine interest in the questions they ask you?
- Do they seem eager to learn?
- Do they seem like a well-rounded person?
- Are they well groomed and dressed neatly?

QUICK STEPS: *PICKING THE RIGHT SALESPERSON.*

Quirky salespeople may be good—not always, but more times than not. Many salespeople are a bit quirky—sometimes more than a bit. Their eccentricities frequently help them connect with customers and make sales. So take their quirkiness into account.

Look for energy. Are they engaging? Positive? Confidant? Willing to go the extra mile?

Great salespeople are a rare blend of ego and empathy. Too much ego leads to arrogance and destruction. Too little empathy leads to the inability to understand your customer and build genuine trust. You want someone who is confident and cares about others and wants to better their customer's lives by giving them a solution represented by your company's products and services.

Remember, the people you are enlisting in your downline will be representing you.

Since you'll have to work closely with them, make sure that you feel comfortable with them and confident that they will build a solid downline for you with integrity and not with over-inflated promises just to get a sale.

Chemistry

Sometimes, you have immediate chemistry. There's a spark. You like this person instantly, want to be involved with him or her, and feel sure that the relationship will work. When that occurs, trust your instincts—they're usually right.

To choose a partner or hire someone, use the Travel Test, which I've used over the years. Ask yourself, "Would I want to sit next to this person for hours on a cross-country plane flight?"

You don't have to be a great friend, obviously, but you have to have a sense if the person is warm, genuine and trustworthy. Are they personable?

Do they seem to have social intelligence? In direct selling, social intelligence and skills are critical. They are the key to success.

Specific Skills

Today, network marketers must be computer literate. List the specific computer skills you want in your ideal candidate and the level you need. For example, do they understand the basics of websites, social networking and simple internet marketing strategies? Do they use Twitter?

QUICK STEPS: *GET GREAT BY BEING GREAT.*

If you want to attract great people to work with you, be great. If you want people who are trustworthy, diligent and fair, be the same. Set the example you want them to follow through you actions, not just through words.

21

Getting Started as a Distributor

In our conversations, Jimmy outlined four important steps that should be taken before a person becomes a network-marketing distributor. They are:

1. ***List Your Goals***

    Be specific. Put in <u>writing</u> exactly how much money you want to make each month for the next two years. It's easy to dismiss setting goals because you have probably heard to do so, so many times. Earl Nightingale, who inspired Jimmy, had this to say about goals: "All you have to do is know where you're going. The answers will come to you of their own accord."

    Push yourself.

    List how much money you're willing to invest in your new business to reach your goals. Don't play it safe or be conservative, set several lofty but realistic goals that are achievable and push yourself to reach them.

    All you need is the plan, the road map, and the courage to press on to your destination.

    As a Depression-era child, Earl Nightingale was hungry for knowledge. From the time he was a young boy, he would frequent the Long Beach Public Library in California, searching for the answer to the question, "How can a person, starting from scratch, who has no particular advantage in the world, reach the goals that he feels are important to him, and by so doing, make a major contribution to others?" His desire to find an answer, coupled with his natural curiosity about the world and its workings spurred him to become one of the world's foremost experts on success and what makes people successful.

(Source: MarkVictorHansen.COM)

Go get my *Speed to Your Wealth Action Plan* to get the exact steps needed to reach your goals. Here is the link: **www.7stepstowealthsystem.com.**

2. *Your daily commitment*

List the amount of time you will devote to your business. Be specific. Break it down by days and hours. Be realistic and make sure to give yourself sufficient time to do all your work well. Remember, in the beginning, your work will go more slowly, but once you get the hang of it, it will go faster.

Here is what Earl Nightingale has to say:

Have you ever wondered why so many people work so hard and honestly without ever achieving anything in particular, and why others don't seem to work hard, yet seem to get everything? They seem to have the "magic touch." You've heard people say, "Everything he touches turns to gold." Have you ever noticed that a person who becomes successful tends to continue to become more successful? And, on the other hand, have you noticed how someone who's a failure tends to continue to fail?

The difference is goals. People with goals succeed because they know where they're going. It's that simple. Failures, on the other hand, believe that their lives are shaped by circumstances ... by things that happen to them ... by exterior forces.

Think of a ship with the complete voyage mapped out and planned. The captain and crew know exactly where the ship is going and how long it will take—it has a definite goal. And 9,999 times out of 10,000, it will get there.

Now let's take another ship—just like the first—only let's not put a crew on it, or a captain at the helm. Let's give it no aiming point, no goal, and no destination. We just start the engines and let it go. I think you'll agree that if it gets out of the harbor at all, it will either sink or wind up on some deserted beach—a derelict. It can't go anyplace because it has no destination and no guidance.

(Source: Nightingale, Earl. Nightingale Conant. <http://www.nightingale.com/AE_Article~i~22~ article~StrangestSecret.aspx>)

3. *List 200 prospects*

List the names and contact information for 200 people who might buy your goods or service or become your distributors.

Don't prejudge or prequalify any of them; just list the name of anyone who comes to your mind. If you edit your list, you'll limit your success.

When you compile your list, imagine that you'll receive money for every name you include—because you will.

To make your list, run through your address and contact files. It could jog your memory and remind you of people who you haven't been in contact with for a while. If you can't find anyone that you list, track him or her down.

4. *List 10 potential leaders*

Write down the names of 10 key people who could be leaders.

Look for those who are good with people, have lots of friends and contacts, and are good networkers.

Find people who really excite you, who are positive and have the potential to be very successful.

Follow carefully Earl Nightingale's recommendations from *The Strangest Secret* that Jimmy Smith read over and over to reprogram his mind for success:

30-Day Action Ideas for Putting *The Strangest Secret* to Work for You

For the next 30 days follow each of these steps every day until you have achieved your goal.

1. Write on a card what it is you want more that anything else. It may be more money. Perhaps you'd like to double your income or make a specific amount of money. It may be a beautiful home. It may be success at your job. It may be a particular position in life. It could be a more harmonious family.

   Write down on your card specifically what it is you want. Make sure it's a single goal and clearly defined. You needn't show it to anyone, but carry it with you so that you can look at it several times a day. Think about it in a cheerful, relaxed, positive way each morning when you get up, and immediately you have something to work for—something to get out of bed for, something to live for.

   Look at it every chance you get during the day and just before going to bed at night. As you look at it, remember that you must become what you think about, and since you're thinking about your goal, you realize that soon it will be yours. In fact, it's really yours the moment you write it down and begin to think about it.

2. Stop thinking about what it is you fear. Each time a fearful or negative thought comes into your mind, replace it with a mental picture of your positive and worthwhile goal. And there will come a time when you'll feel like giving up. It's easier for a human being to think negatively than positively. That's why only five percent are successful! You must begin now to place yourself in that group.

   "Act as though it were impossible to fail," as Dorothea Brande said. No matter what your goal—if you've kept your goal before you every day—you'll wonder and marvel at this new life you've found.

3. Your success will always be measured by the quality and quantity of service you render. Most people will tell you that they want to

make money, without understanding this law. The only people who make money work in a mint. The rest of us must earn money. This is what causes those who keep looking for something for nothing, or a free ride, to fail in life. Success is not the result of making money; earning money is the result of success—and success is in direct proportion to our service.

Most people have this law backwards. It's like the man who stands in front of the stove and says to it: "Give me heat and then I'll add the wood." How many men and women do you know, or do you suppose there are today, who take the same attitude toward life? There are millions.

We've got to put the fuel in before we can expect heat. Likewise, we've got to be of service first before we can expect money. Don't concern yourself with the money. Be of service ... build ... work ... dream ... create! Do this and you'll find there is no limit to the prosperity and abundance that will come to you.

Don't start your test until you've made up your mind to stick with it. If you should fail during your first 30 days—by that I mean suddenly find yourself overwhelmed by negative thoughts—simply start over again from that point and go 30 more days. Gradually, your new habit will form, until you find yourself one of that wonderful minority to whom virtually nothing is impossible.

Above all ... don't worry! Worry brings fear, and fear is crippling. The only thing that can cause you to worry during your test is trying to do it all yourself. Know that all you have to do is hold your goal before you; everything else will take care of itself.

Take this 30-day test, then repeat it ... then repeat it again. Each time it will become more a part of you until you'll wonder how you could have ever have lived any other way. Live this new way and the floodgates of abundance will open and pour over you more riches than you may have dreamed existed. Money? Yes, lots of it. But what's more important, you'll have peace ... you'll be in that wonderful minority who lead calm, cheerful, successful lives.

(Source: Nightingale, Earl. Nightingale Conant. < http://www.nightingale.com/AE_Article~i~22 ~article~StrangestSecret.aspx>)

The Tools of Your Trade

To operate your business efficiently, you need to have the right tools and follow the right steps. Here are some essentials:

1. *Phone system*

   Get a good phone and voicemail system. Put in a separate phone line for your network-marketing business. Be sure that you can access it remotely and that it has conferencing capability.

   To keep costs down, some people only use a cell phone. I recommend you have a land line because the connection is clearer. I have always had at least two lines and a call waiting feature so if my two lines were busy, I could hit flash on one of the lines and get the third call.

2. *Website*

   Set up your website and familiarize yourself with its help and support areas and its features. Log on to your website and examine everything that visitors will be able to access. Try each feature to make sure that they all work well, are easy to navigate and are user friendly. Check all links. Know all about your website so you can talk intelligently about it with your prospects.

   Network-marketing companies today like Isagenix® give you the ability to set up your own website within their system and set up your entire back office for handling your sign-up of customers and distributors. They give you access to numerous online training materials including subjects that cover marketing and sales strategies and techniques.

As I have emphasized, this type of setup should be your baseline—your starting point from which to build your own unique network-marketing business.

You can attract a following by learning how to set up a fan page on Facebook or by learning the ins and outs of Twitter and "Tweeting." You can give your potential clients and existing customers additional information to help better their lives

View your website as your business within a business—that of your direct selling company. Follow your direct selling company's rules, but realize there are ways to be creative and distinguish yourself on the Web. In addition to your website, make sure you have a blog since this is a way for people to get to know you as a person.

3. *Supplies*

Review the direct selling company's product list and then order the necessary supplies, promotional materials, stationery, and business cards. Have all necessary supplies and promotional materials on hand before you actually try to conduct business.

Make sure you review carefully the supplies available to you from your direct selling company. They most likely have spent a lot of time and money developing and testing them. You can learn a great deal from studying what they give you. Don't just mechanically get stuff and then start selling. Understand fully what you are marketing and selling. Learn from your sponsors and the company what steps work and in what sequence. The sequence and order you do things, similar to baking a cake, makes the difference between success and failure.

4. *Meet with your sponsors*

Meet with your sponsor to set your goals. Then work together to develop business-building plans and strategies to reach those goals. Listen to their advice and make sure that you are on the same page.

5. *Upline communications*

   Determine how you will keep in touch with your upline.

   Do they prefer email, the phone or other communications?

   Is there a chain of command that they want you to go through? Maintain regular contact with your sponsors and make sure that you are receiving all new information from the corporate office.

6. *Attend local meetings* Whenever possible, attend and participate in local group's meetings. Build a strong local base of people in your community who will support you. Become a part of your local community.

7. *New Distributors*

Work closely with each new distributor you sponsor and show them the ropes. Help them follow each of these steps I have listed above.

22

Five Superstars

Here's the secret to becoming a huge direct selling success: find five superstars, according to Jimmy.

If you recruit five fabulous producers for your downline, they will put you on the map. They will enable you to earn a large, steady income stream.

Just look at the math. If you bring in five superstars and each one recruits two more, you'll have 10 people working for you. Soon you'll have 20, 40 and so on. As each of your distributors' downlines grow geometrically, they become a part of your downline. So your downline will snowball in size. As it does, you'll get a cut of what each of your distributors and all their distributors make.

While almost everyone focuses on recruiting numerous people, Jimmy and other top 1% network marketers focus on sifting through their recruits to find five superstars.

To be successful, you don't need hundreds of people in your downline. You only need literally a handful of distributors who are go-getters and produce. Quality is far more important than quantity.

In order to find five superstars, you may have to try out 100 or 200 people, but if you find one or two superstars, you'll be well on your way. Then, keep going through another 100 to 200 until you find the core five.

When you have five superstar distributors in your downline, it's the equivalent of having an annuity or a license to make money. They will create leverage by doing the recruiting for you and your earnings will compound. When you have five superstars in place, your biggest job will be to keep them motivated and not slowing their pace.

As you build your downline, you move into the **leadership development business.** Just as your up line sponsors lead you, you lead your superstars. You feed the engine, see that it always has gas, that it's well lubricated and finely tuned. Your focus will be to keep your money machine running smoothly ahead. And when it is, enjoy the ride to the bank.

The Natural Sales Stars Myth

You don't have to be a great natural salesperson to be a network-marketing star.

It's more important to know how to pick outstanding salespeople who will build great downlines. Picture yourself as the producer of your own *American Idol* show. When looking to build your downline and find your five superstars, you are doing what Simon Cowell and Randy Jackson do. You are putting on auditions to find your top five to compete for your prize— being part of your downline. Remember, the top five get a lot of publicity, recognition and money.

Your most important job is to find superstar distributors, people who will make money for themselves, the company and you. And when you find them, nurture them, develop them and get them up to speed.

Make them experts on your goods or services, see that they are well organized, and know your company's systems, payment plan, products, materials, culture and strategies. Become the system expert, the person with all the answers, who everything runs through.

When you have five superstars in your downline, you'll be light-years ahead of everyone else. While your competitors will be working on one or two cylinders, you'll be cruising on five. Then, as more come on board, you'll gain so much horsepower that you'll soon be moving at hyper-speed. Before long, your multi-pronged attack will have you in that top 1% of network marketers and part of the elite 1% richest in the world club.

More Options

As you move to the top of the mountain, look around. Try to spot ways to diversify and find fertile new fields to plow. From your lofty vantage point, many interesting new options may appear. Everybody loves a winner, so you may receive interesting offers. And, because of your success, you may be in an excellent position to take advantage of them.

The key is not to lose focus on how you got to be successful. Always feed and maintain your base or downline. Don't get smug or complacent.

Try to have several options going simultaneously. I always like to have a multiple stream of income strategy. Start by exploring various new opportunities to increase your downline and to find those with the best fit or potential. Get leads for your sponsors, distributors, customers and suppliers. Keep your ear to the ground.

Now that you're on top, you probably have the luxury to branch out, examine your options, implement some of them and let them develop and mature. But do not go off into ventures that are outside your expertise or that could in any way undermine or jeopardize your base business.

Go Where the Fish Are Biting

Keep one base or focal point and leverage it in many different ways.

For example, write an article on your network-marketing products. Then repurpose or create many different ways to communicate the content in your article. Here are some of the ways you can communicate to others with your content:

1. Blogs

2. Podcasts

3. Videos

4. Audios

5. More detailed reports

6. A book

7. A newsletter or e-zine

8. Print or Internet columns

9. Tests, quizzes or games

QUICK STEPS: *RECRUIT BABY BOOMERS.*

In your search to find superstars, be open to all possibilities, people of all ages and from all groups. Remember that Jimmy didn't start with Isagenix® until he was 74.

Don't overlook Baby Boomers. They can be an excellent fit. The baby boomer generation is aging and many boomers face the prospect of outliving their assets. Many have been highly successful and still have a lot left in their tank. Some may be bored and itching for something new. These vital, experienced individuals may want a home-based business, sources of extra money that have low entry costs and involve little risk.

Boomers are well connected, which makes them ideal for direct selling. They can be a fertile source for your downline. Just imagine if you had five Jimmy Smiths as distributors. You would be on easy street!

Roger Barnett, Chairman and CEO of Shaklee Corporation, a multi-level marketing company that sells a wide range of nutrition products, emphasized the need to develop business models and health opportunities for the 78 million aging baby boomers, some of whom will began turning 60 in January 2006. "The public and private sectors need to work together to develop policies that will help the aging baby boomers remain a productive and engaged part of society."

23

Practical Steps for Success

Like Jimmy, I built my business by networking in person and by phone. For me, nothing beats personal contact, whether it be face-to-face or voice-to-voice. I find that email, texting or other online communications is not as personal or as intimate. They don't enable you to build as close bonds.

That said, how you communicate is generational. While my generation emails, younger people text. Texting is their medium, how they communicate. They find email and phoning passé; it's not their thing. So if you want to reach them, text.

In reality, you want to communicate using the net and cell phones and then meet in person such as events to build deeper relationships.

Jimmy's Formula: Take Action and Succeed

"A tried and true formula for building any business is *plan your work and then work your plan*," Jimmy told me. "Sounds simple enough, but the problem with getting the plan done is *your attitude*. How many of us say, 'I'll get to it when I get a chance?' You know what that means? You will never get to it unless someone lights a fire under your backside! Well, why not *try self-ignition?*"

Jimmy outlined eight simple, but proven, ways to kick the procrastination habit and get your work done. Here they are:

1. *Break it down*. When tasks seem overwhelming, break them into small parts that can be more easily completed. If you attack it as one big project, it can be intimidating and you won't know where to start. Then, once you get going, you could easily get lost. So, divide the project into manageable chunks. Then assign a specific deadline (date and time) to each part and attack them systematically.

2. *Write it down*. Make your goals official by writing them on paper. The top 1% of entrepreneurs and investors advocate writing down your business plan and your specific goals. When you do, and especially when you write them by hand, you bypass your defense mechanisms and activate the right side of your brain, which is the more intuitive imaginative part of your mind. By accessing the right side of your brain you set your subconscious in motion to find creative ways to accomplish your specific goals.

3. *Talk it out.* Tell the world about your goals. Broadcast it; get the word out, let people know what your goals are. When you do, your friends and associates will ask you how it's going, which should motivate you. Once you tell others your goals, it becomes a commitment, you increase your investment in completing it and you put yourself on the line. If we don't follow through, we subject ourselves to embarrassment and even ridicule. When we tell others we may also elicit their support and the contribution of their resources to help us reach our goals.

4. *Consistency.* Establish a regular time each day to attend to specific tasks. Put aside time to make phone calls, to answer emails, make appointments, write reports and to attend to other specific jobs. At first, set modest targets and see how it works. Then make the changes that seem appropriate. If you plan to make ten calls, make them every day. Pretty soon, you may decide to make 15 or cut your calls to seven. Or, you can find that you can make more calls in less time. Stick with your schedule religiously. Whatever number of calls you decide to make, be sure to make them all. Build discipline and sooner or later, it will pay off.

5. *Organize.* At your workspace, place everything where you can easily reach it. Put those things you use most the closest to you. Become more efficient and if you have everything you need at your fingertips, you will. Organize your business. See Appendix 1, Gary's Home Office Organizing Tips, at the back of this book and follow these steps:

   a. <u>Start with the end in mind</u>. Visualize yourself serving a customer who purchased from you. Now, work your way backwards from that purchase and note all the steps you went through since you first came in contact with that customer.

   b. <u>Tools and resources</u>. Determine the tools and resources you'll need to serve your customer or your distributor. Make a written list and review and update it periodically.

   c. <u>Fulfillment and payments</u>. Know how your direct selling company will deliver products, monitor those in your downline and account to you for payments. Learn how and when you can access and track this information: via regular written reports or online?

   d. <u>Post-sales</u>. Know each step in the post-sales process and who is responsible for each step. Consider it part of your customer service and follow-up. Work this end diligently because it usually translates into happy customers, repeat business and new business referrals.

   e. <u>Organize your home office</u>. When you set up your office, focus on your sales and post-sales. Since they can be your big money makers, organize your office with them in mind. Make sure that you can deliver whatever is needed and answer questions.

   f. <u>List what you need</u>. Make a list of all items you will need in your home office to make the entire process work from beginning to end. For example, all sales tools, agreements, product information, forms and contact information.

6. _Give rewards._ Reward yourself for meeting your goals. Plan your rewards ahead so that you'll have something to look forward to. Give yourself rewards for meeting your small, medium and large goals or on whatever other basis you decide. Don't make any reward too big to be attainable or too small to motivate you. Try to select rewards that excite you and that you'll work to get.

7. _Visible goals._ Post your goals where you can easily see them. Make them visible because just mentally knowing them may not be enough of a reminder. Put your deadlines and the rewards for achieving your goals with the reminders. Some people like to put inspirational messages with their reminders.

8. _Business before pleasure._ Give yourself incentives by making something that you normally do and enjoy contingent on the completion of specific work. For example, don't go out for coffee until you fill out your monthly progress report. If you build discipline and develop a strong work ethic, you won't be easily diverted and will be able to get more work done well in less time.

Knowing the steps to follow in order to succeed is just the start. You have to follow them. That's the tough part. Following them can be hard—especially doing so on a regular basis. The key is to stick to it and try not to stray. It may be hard at first, but through discipline and repetition, you'll soon get the knack. After a while, it will begin to feel natural. It will become liberating and since you're so well organized, you'll have more spare time.

Don't cheat! If you do, you'll not only be kidding yourself—but harming yourself as well.

QUICK STEPS: *WATCH YOUR HABITS.*

Often, they reveal your destructive habits or addictions. Addictions such as smoking, drugs, sex, work, alcohol, eating and gambling can kill your business and ruin your life

You may be the best-organized person on Earth, but if you have addictions, they can kill your business and you. Addictions are not just distractions; they remove you from your work. Once you're away, it's harder to get back and it costs you more time. When you're pressed for time, it becomes more difficult to do everything well.

You may or may not be aware of the full impact your addictions have on your life. They are very difficult to get rid of, but facing them rather than ignoring their effect on your life and business is a step in the right direction.

24

Distributors' Top 10 Secrets

The top 10 reasons why network-marketing distributors succeed are:

1. *Goals*. Successful people set realistic yet challenging goals, and focus on them. They understand that rejection is a part of a constructive learning process and never, never give up. Succeeding in business is often a product of your mind-set, your perseverance, desire and will. It takes strength, will power and tenacity and always focusing on your goals.

2. *Mastery*. The most successful people have a complete, encyclopedic understanding of their entire product line and the company compensation plan. They're experts on their goods and services. They can effectively articulate that knowledge and share it with distributors and prospects.

3. *Spread the word.* They take every opportunity to tell others about the company's products and business opportunities. Let people know what you are doing and why. Show your confidence and belief in your self and the company. Being shy, fearful or reluctant will get you nowhere and speaking up will motivate you

4. *Seminars*. Winners know the importance of knowledge and information. They take every opportunity to learn more about the direct selling business by attending seminars, reading industry publications, watching videos and listening to CDs. They understand

that continual education is essential to getting ahead; you can't get to the top without it. Learn baby learn!

5. *Meetings*. Top producers regularly attend and participate in meetings with other distributors. Face-to-face meetings build personal relationships and team spirit. It's fun to socialize, make friends, talk shop and find ways to collaborate. Don't underestimate the benefits of these relationships and how much it helps when people know, like and respect you. People like to know and deal with successful people and will go out of their way to help them.

   Get out and meet people; boost your profile. Communicate. Learn. Let people know you exist and you are committed. If you're active, aggressive, it will motivate your upline and the company to mentor you and teach you how to be even more successful. After all, it's in their best interests.

6. *Websites*. Top network marketers use their and the company's website to keep informed and keep others informed. Smart network-marketing companies recognize the power of the Web to communicate their ideas and brand while helping their distributors to sell more.

   What Jimmy likes is that Isagenix® offers a complete suite of products and a back office support. So, distributors like Jimmy can keep track of their business and their downlines. The company also provides excellent instructional material to their distributors. Generally, they give information products and information on recruiting and educating customers.

7. *Communicate regularly*. They stay in touch with everyone in their upline and their downline. Exchange ideas and provide training, support and encouragement. Set goals. With all of our electronic tools, it's easy to communicate and it is usually fun. Share your ideas; be cooperative and collaborative because it builds relationships, trust, bonds and loyalty.

8. *Following up*. The top network marketers make courteous, regular follow-up calls to their prospects. Few people buy or sign up as a

distributor on the first, second or third contacts. It usually takes multiple calls. According to studies, people see a product or offer at least seven times before they buy. Chapter 27 discusses following up in greater detail.

9. *Promotional tools.* They make use of the free promotional tools furnished by their companies so they can send professional looking packages.

   For instance, Isagenix® materials are informative, reader friendly and extremely professional looking. They are excellent materials. They have a consistent design and brand theme, so all of the Isagenix® products tie together.

   Many network-marketing companies' product lines lack a consistent theme, look or brand. One product does not look like the other.

   Isagenix®'s line, for example, doesn't look helter-skelter. Its packaging is consistent: a white background and uplifting colors convey a feeling of energy and well-being.

10. *Upline support.* They bring their sponsors in on three-way calls and meetings with prospects and potential distributors. They're open, want to learn and will go to their upline, their sponsors and ask, "What do I have to do? How should I prepare?"

Successful network marketers have similar traits as other top performers—those in the top 1%. They had excellent teachers who put them through the rigorous learning process called deliberate practice. They practiced over and over until they mastered the most challenging parts of their business.

Think of weight lifters. A teacher pushes them to lift increasing amounts of weight, shows them the proper procedure and stands by as they lift. When a target weight is lifted, the teacher pushes the lifter to the next level and the process continues until the lifter reaches his or her potential. When that pattern is repeated continually, it's deliberate practice.

Since everything changes, it's challenging to know when to keep going, when to change course or quit. Those decisions become far easier when you know your goals and what you ultimately want.

25
Selling

Sales entail overcoming a series of hurdles and objections until you find the right people and they feel comfortable enough with you to buy.

Direct selling expert Bryan Tracy believes that a new business has to spend 80% of its time on sales. Everything you do in your business—preparation, practice, and trial and error—must be broken down so you can operate at top efficiency. In direct selling, 80% of your time should be devoted to sales.

Selling is a complex process that has been studied and analyzed. Everyone has their own theory and some of them actually work.

I've spent my life in sales, and I've learned that to be successful, each person must develop his or her own approach but still follow certain fundamentals and principles that are common to the best salespeople. At first, selling may seem unnatural and uncomfortable. You have to build a script that works for you.

To understand how to build a winning script, you need to recognize that selling has changed. Why? The speed of information and the scarcity of attention. You cannot sell people by interrupting them and being pushy. You need to establish a relationship and trust with people first, as I have pointed out.

Now when you try to sell customers, you must be their advisor and consultant. They must think of you as their ally, as a member of their team. You must be seen as being on their side, not someone who is merely trying to sell them.

Today, people have so many choices that they can't be pushed or hoodwinked like before, though there is no complete insulation from con men. Because unscrupulous salespeople exist in great numbers, people need to be given enough time and information to make up their own minds. Today, it's not about selling—it's about why people buy.

People like buying. They also need to buy, but they hate being sold. They also have problems and will pay to have them solved. So examine your tactics and your approach to give potential buyers what they want and need—not what you want to sell.

Jimmy Says: I never, ever sell anything and I don't try to sell anything. I'm not in the sales business. I share. I share my experience, strength and hope with people. I share my story. In sales, facts tell and stories sell. Stories will always sell over anything else. You should tell your story and kindly offer these products to someone. You want them to try the products. You want them to feel as good as you feel about them… I know the product works like a charm for 95% of the people who use it correctly. People lose weight. They feel great. Some people have lost a hundred pounds, two hundred pounds; we have one customer who lost three hundred pounds. I know these products work. They worked for me.

Here is what I say to people: "Stay on these products for three months, almost 100 days, and if you don't feel 100 percent better at the end of three months, I will personally give you every penny back." That is how sure I am that these products work.

Once he knew that the product worked, that was a powerful motivation to go out there and sell it. Plus, he adds, "More important than just working, I felt so good. I felt and looked 15 years younger and people told me that."

Instead of selling, Jimmy takes another approach. He:

- Points customers and distributors to solutions and benefits
- Lets them sample products
- Gives them information and
- Lets them make up their own minds.

Some people who are reluctant to go into direct selling say, "I don't know that many people, or I don't want to sell to just my friends and family." But they don't have to. As I have pointed out to you, technology has made it unnecessary to hit on your family and friends.

The Internet, cell phones, Twitter and social networks have opened up a whole new world of potential distributors and customers. They can broaden your influence and let you reach people *all over the world.*

Multi-level marketing has been transformed by the Internet. Jimmy Smith thought the wellness industry was perfect for network marketing, even before the Internet. He was participating in two industries that are on their way to becoming trillion-dollar industries. The Internet's ecommerce industry will soon be a multi-trillion-dollar industry, the biggest marketplace in the history of the world.

When you put these three trends together, opportunities are created like never before. If you're in any one of those trends, you're in good shape. If you're in two, you're in better shape. Now you can take part in all three. Jimmy's in the wellness industry, network marketing and e-commerce. He asks his friends, "How can you fail?"

The Jimmy Smith Winning Sales Process

Jimmy prefers the friendly approach. He will call a prospect and say, "How are you doing, how's that family, how are things going with you, how's your wife, what's happening to you?"

By asking questions, Jimmy learns where his prospect is and what is going on in his or her life. He doesn't start pitching right away. He starts a conversation because he's focused upon building a relationship and rapport.

In each conversation with a prospect, more information about the prospect and his or her life is disclosed. Note that information and keep it in your files. Then when you contact that individual again, ask him or her about it.

When the conversation gets going, Jimmy switches gears. His approach is friendly not pushy. He says, "You won't believe the company I've found. I've lost 21 pounds and four inches off my waist using two nine-day systems in only 18 days. Is that not unbelievable?" Then he gives them time to respond. Usually, they say, "That sure is!"

Jimmy then continues by saying, "I feel great, I feel younger, I look younger," he declares. "People tell me I look younger. I have more energy than I've had in years."

At that point, most people show interest. They ask, "What's the product and who makes it?" That gives Jimmy permission; they open the door.

Only then does Jimmy talk about the product and state how great it is. Until then he was simply describing his own experience. When the prospect shows interest, Jimmy will ask if he or she would like to try the product. He wants the person to have a positive experience with the product, and Jimmy begins that experience by being friendly.

Free—The Golden Ticket to Success

Get your customers' or distributors' attention by giving them something they value.

It can be free information or tools that your company provides.

When you give them those items, include your website address. Get their commitment to look at it. This is the get-acquainted approach. Then follow up to answer their questions.

If a car salesperson wants to sell you my car, he/she offers to let you test-drive it. That's their free offer. If you drive the car and like it, then they try to close the sale. If they can, they try to sell you add-ons including financing, insurance, undercoating, which is where the real money is—the back end.

The objective in McDonald's is to sell you the extras or back end after you have purchased the front-end hamburger. You go into McDonald's for a burger and then are up-sold to fries, soda and dessert. And when you go to a supermarket, what about all those free handouts that are intended to make you buy?

Today, giving free stuff is key. Learn what free stuff your company gives away including tools. One of the great appeals of direct selling is that the companies give you most of what you need to market and sell their products. This includes free brochures, training videos, payment plan expectations and back office systems such as accounting, websites.

Free is powerful. Free samples. Free giveaways. Free brochures. Free tools.

QUICK STEPS: *GIVE PEOPLE **FREE STUFF** TO CREATE RELATIONSHIPS AND TRUST FIRST, THEN SALES.*

To get people to trust what you are offering, let them test-drive it. Give them a sample or let them try it out. Let them actually taste what they will be getting and see how it works. When you let people sample, your goods and services speak for themselves. People don't feel that they're being sold, but that they're deciding for themselves.

Take Your Time to Develop Your Relationship

Those who go for the quick hit usually fail quickly. Don't immediately push for the sale or think of each prospect as a mark and try to make fast money.

The sales process is a series of interactions to build trust and on-going relationships.

Start with a low-key exploration of what the customers or distributors previously experienced. Find out what they want to accomplish in a year.

If those prospects do not sign up, don't abandon them. After a reasonable time, follow up.

Let them make the decision to buy—don't try to sell them.

First, capture your prospects' attention. Then if they get comfortable with you, they may buy. Don't give up quickly. Keep trying and following up.

The true art of sales is in the follow up. Most people need to hear your message a minimum of seven times—sometimes, up to 28 times before they will buy. Find ways to communicate consistently with both your prospects and your existing customers (the Internet makes this much easier for you!).

Systematize

Create an automated online business system through networking. Here's how:

Consider the products you market as a bundle of potential information. For example, Isagenix®'s products consist of:

1. Formulations of ingredients that provide certain information
2. Each ingredient itself is information
3. The benefits of these formulations.
4. The packaging and presentation of that information and:
   a. Giving some of it away free
   b. Charging a small amount to get more information out

This concept is at the heart of information marketing. They sell a low-priced item to cover their advertising costs and sell the more expensive back-end products for a profit.

The income you receive from selling this low-cost front end information should cover your cost of marketing or advertising. This is called a self-liquidating offer (SLO) because your sales revenue covers your advertising cost to recruit customers and/or distributors. When people buy from you and are satisfied, they want to purchase your more expensive products and join your downline.

The Numbers

Set up a system that lets you instantly know your numbers, exactly how well your business is doing down to the last penny. Have your system set up to reflect all areas of your business. Then you can quickly find the areas that are doing well and those that are falling short so you can promptly attend to them.

At all times, know your real cost of doing business, how much you're taking in and the amount of your profit. We all have expenses, businesses and individuals, every day. If we don't know our numbers, we don't know how much we can afford to spend, invest or save. Since the purpose of any business is to make money, know your bottom line or you won't be in business very long.

Some people are intimidated by numbers. But today numbers are easy to calculate. Most of business is simple math you learned in sixth grade. Warren Buffett says, "If I can't figure out the numbers with simple math, then there's something wrong with the transaction."

Jimmy Smith uses basic math that he learned as a butcher. If you are afraid of numbers, take a simple calculator and put in some numbers. Try to translate what you are currently doing into numbers. Take your daily expenses. Start breaking down what you do into numbers. You may already be doing this! Soon your fear or hesitancy will go away.

Why Top Network Marketers Succeed

Let's take a look at the reason top network marketers achieve success. Notice that many of the criteria are the same for succeeding in life in general and in social networking on Facebook or LinkedIn.

1. *Likeability*—They like people and people like them. Direct selling is a people business. It involves personal interaction and building relationships—often with a number of people.

2. *Trust*—People respond faster and make greater commitments when they trust those with whom they are dealing.

3. *Competence*—We all feel more secure with those who have demonstrated the ability to execute and deliver on their promises.

4. *Warmth*—Warmth is comforting because people sense it comes from the heart. It tells them that you're genuine, sincere, which allays their doubts and fears.

5. *Sharing*—Sharing reflects generosity, the willingness to help and give. It's a part of our learning process where you give to help others succeed.

6. *Leadership*—In the end, it's all about leadership and leadership development. People like to follow those they admire, believe in and trust. It inspires them and helps them learn.

7. *Self-confidence*—It's reassuring and gives other confidence that you will deliver on what you say. People are drawn to confidence and move away from insecurity and desperation.

8. *Self-discipline*—Others are impressed by your ability to focus and stay on point. They admire how you organize your knowledge and skills so your time, energy and resources are used efficiently and effectively.

9. *Products*—First they like and trust you, and then that carries over to your products. If your products consistently deliver, you will get the repeat business.

10. *Company*—Successful people choose the right companies with which to associate, companies that support them with excellent products, training and sales materials and customer focus.

11. *Value*—You deliver items that people want and feel are worth the price.

QUICK STEPS: *LEARN SOFT SKILLS.*

It may seem frustrating that there is no simple magic bullet to success. But this is a huge advantage since your success depends more and more on how you are perceived by others as a whole person. This is very advantageous for women, since they are excellent at relating to the whole person.

What Causes Network Marketers to Fail?

Most network marketers fail because they use outdated approaches that no longer work.

They try to sell, not to serve. As I have underscored, people don't want to be sold, but they do like to buy. Many salespeople don't understand their customers, and many don't even try to understand their wants and needs. They do not listen. They talk and only hear themselves.

They make assumptions about them that are usually wrong. Most salespeople don't try to get permission to sell.

They lead with the products instead of engaging potential customers, trying to build relationships with them and gaining their trust.

Customers want their problems solved.

They want their needs fulfilled and they want the best value. Salespeople have to understand their customers' needs and problems, and then offer them goods and service that will fulfill their needs, solve their problems and be good values.

In writing copy on your website or in other forms of advertisement to attract customers and/or distributors for your downline, here are some great tips by a top marketing consultant:

- Focus your advertising's message on the benefits and applications of your products or services. Then let the layout and design of your ads enhance your company's image.

- **Put Benefits in Your Headlines**

  If you put a benefit in the headline you'll have a better chance of catching the reader's attention and generating an inquiry or request for more information. If after reading the headline a reader can ask "so what?" you probably described a feature instead of a benefit. The answer to "so what?" is probably the benefit.

- **Talk About Applications**

  If your product or service is ideal for specific applications, say so. When readers recognize their application for your product or service they will be more likely to respond...

- **Make Them an Offer They Can't Refuse**

  If you want your prospects to respond, you have to give them a convincing reason to do so. Keep the phrase "what's in it for me?" in mind as you're writing your ad's call to action. It's what your prospects are thinking as they decide whether or not they will take the time or effort to respond...

- **Choose Your Words Carefully**

  The word "free" is a powerful inquiry generator. Everyone wants something for nothing. Direct marketers have long known the power of this word. Take a look at just about any direct response ad and you'll see it used.

  "New" is another word that is sure to attract attention and generate more inquiries. Legally, however, you can only use "new" if it is new, and only for a limited period of time (usually 6 months). Check with your legal advisor.

- **Talk First Person With The Reader**

  Use words in your copy like "you" and "your" to focus on the readers' needs rather than boasting about how good "we" and "our" products or services are. For example, the statement "You will get the work done 25% quicker" is much stronger than "Our product is 25% faster than the competition."

- **Ask for the Order**

  Any experienced salesperson can tell you, you won't get the order unless you ask for it.

  Create benefit-oriented offers such as "call, write, fax, e-mail or visit our Web site today

- **Give Them a Compelling Reason to Inquire Right Away**

  You'll get more inquiries if you design your offer to reward those who inquire right away. For example, try something like "If you are one of the first 500 to inquire, we'll also send you a free booklet entitled, "fifteen ways to cut your inventory costs.""...

- **Mention Your Website**

  Make it clear to readers that they can get the rest of the story about your products or services instantly by visiting your Web site. Then make sure your Web site makes it easy for them to find this information."

(Source: "16 proven techniques for better B2B sales leads generation with print advertising" M. H. "Mac" McIntosh, CBC. Mac McIntosh. <http://www.sales-lead-experts.com/tips/articles/print-advertising.cfm>)

26

Testimonials and Referrals

A few weeks to a month after you sell your goods or services to customers, call them. Ask if they've used your items and whether they're working well. Tell them that you just want to make sure that they're happy and definitely don't try to sell. You may even want to put together a short list of questions to ask about their satisfaction with your items, how well they work, your company's service and their feelings about the buying process.

Consider these calls customer service and a way to build your customer relations and good will. If your customers inform you about any problems, immediately try to have them fixed. Demonstrate to your customers that their satisfaction is very important to you.

Keep in contact with your customers periodically to confirm that they're still satisfied. After a few calls, ask them to write testimonials for you expressing their satisfaction. Have them write a letter on their stationery describing their feelings about your product and their experience dealing with you and your company.

Post testimonials on your website and keep the hard copies to show prospects. Audio and video testimonials can also be extremely effective. When you play them for new prospects, they can build excitement and emotional involvement.

Testimonials can have additional and unexpected benefits. Customers may praise features of your goods or services that you didn't think were important, but that your customer loved. They can state that you excelled in areas that you never gave a second thought to. Testimonials can bring to light competitive advantages that you never recognized.

Ironically, few businesses or individuals know their actual competitive advantages. Only a miniscule percentage know where they're truly stronger than their competition. Few actually are aware of what their customers consider their greatest strengths. Knowing your actual competitive advantages is itself a huge competitive advantage that you can use to build your business. Here is a great outline by top copywriter Brain Keith Voiles on how to effectively use testimonials:

Here is a bunch of tips, hints and ideas about using testimonials:

1. Testimonials can be used effectively in any marketing format:

   - Emails

   - Fax Blasts

   - Websites

   - Live-audio Testimonials on your site

   - Brochures

   - Flyers

   - Business Cards

   - On-Hold Messages For Incoming Calls

   - Video Tape Demonstrations

   - Audio Tape Demonstrations

   - Cover Letters

   - Advertisements

   - Posters

   - Basically anywhere that can be used to induce prospects to take action that will lead to a sell.

2. As a very general rule of thumb, use about two testimonials per page in each of your marketing documents. But that doesn't mean they have to be spread out... sometimes you'll want them all bunched up together. Other times it'll help your copy more to have them spread out.

3. Always get testimonials at every chance you can.

4. Never stop gathering testimonials.

5. Use evaluation forms for EVERY MARKET NICHE that you work. This is perhaps the simplest way to get testimonials.

6. Get testimonials for every benefit that you offer to each market.

7. Testimonials will help you excite your prospects about the benefits that you have to offer, and lower their anxieties about buying from you, because they know that people just like them have received the promised benefits from you.

The Winning Testimonial Formula

"Winning testimonials are benefit packed. They help reduce prospect anxieties and get them excited about buying you.

"Winning testimonials show a prospect that someone just like him has received real benefits from what he is now considering buying. That's what a winning testimonial does.

"Here is the formula stripped down to its bare-butt naked bones just in case it's not obvious to you:

- I am like you.

- I had a problem like you and wanted to achieve the same benefits that you do.

- Like you, I was concerned about what I should do, wondering if anyone could really help.

- Well, now I know. (Your product or service) provided (the benefit I desired). Just like it will do for you!

"Does this formula sound simple? It is. It works, and it works well …give this type of outline to any customer of yours that's crazy about how good a job you do—- or how great your product performs, and have them follow it when they write your letter. "It is benefit packed and tells your prospect that someone like him is out there, that has used you with great success."

(Source: "7 Ways to Use Testimonials & a Few More Tips for You to Use" Brian Keith Voiles. Best Affiliate Products. <www.bestaffiliateproducts.com>)

Referrals

When you ask for a testimonial, also ask for referrals. Say, "Who do you know that might be interested in this company or product? Can I contact them and say that you suggested that I give them a call?" I frequently ask, "Do you really like this product? What do you think of it? Do you have other people that you think might also be interested?"

If the person seems eager to help you, ask them for a personal introduction. For example, say, "Could you call and tell him about me so I don't sound like a salesman making a cold call? Will you also tell him that I will be contacting him?"

Whether someone wants to help you depends upon your relationship to the person you are asking for the referral, and how beneficial they see the referral to be versus the possibility it could backfire if things don't go well.

When people give you referrals, always express your thanks. I prefer to thank them in writing because it shows that I made a special effort. Also think about sending them a gift to show your appreciation. It doesn't have to be expensive or elaborate—just a gesture to say thanks. If you receive a steady stream of referrals from one source, consider giving him or her a bigger gift or even a fee.

Seth Godin, an entrepreneur and well-known author of business books, offers some tips on referrals:

Given the no-win nature of most referrals, you need to reset your expectations and consider a few ideas:

- Make it easy for someone to bring up what you do (by changing the nature of the service or product).

- Give your best customers something of real value to offer to their friends (a secret menu, a significant gift certificate). Once you do that, *not* giving that gift to a friend feels selfish.

- Paying me to refer you rarely works, because you're not just asking for a minute of my time, you're asking me to put my credibility on the line.

- Understand that low-risk referrals happen more often than high-risk ones, and either figure out how to become a low-risk referral or embrace the fact that you have to be truly amazing in order to earn one.

and

- Be worthy. Not just in the work you do, but in your status in the marketplace. I'm far more likely to refer someone with a back story, someone who's an underdog, or relatively unknown. That's why saying "thank you" in deeds (not so much in words) goes such a long way.

(Source: Godin, Seth. "How to Get Referrals." Seth's Blog. <http://sethgodin.typepad.com/seths_blog/2006/11/how_to_get_refe.html>)

27
Following Up

In direct selling, rejection is the biggest obstacle; it's something that you constantly face. When you <u>contact prospects,</u> most of them say no. Some are cruel, abrasive, even nasty and they hang up on you. It can be discouraging and hurt.

When prospects say, "No," don't take it personally. They're not saying no to you, they're saying no to the product or service. Also you may have called them at a bad time. Be prepared for some rejections to be emphatic. If you press them, expect to hear them ask, "What don't you understand about the word no?"

If someone says no, never get into a confrontation—even if you're angry and offended. Just back off and try not to lose the contact. Defuse the situation even if you have to apologize and say that you didn't mean to offend. Be pleasant, calm and understanding. Do what you can to keep the contact alive so you can follow up and contact them again. Try to keep it light and friendly and then ask, "Can I check back with you in a few months to see how you're doing?"

Jimmy has had lots of experience with rejection so he developed a way to win over naysayers. Here's his approach in his own words:

I knew in order to get a yes, I had to get a certain amount of nos. Sometimes you have to get 12—15 nos from the same person before you get a yes. That's called persistence. It's very important in anything you do in life, but especially in sales or network marketing.

The wins built my business. The nos built my character. When you can talk to 30 people and get 30 nos in a row, but keep smiling and dialing until you get a yes, that's character.

I had a fellow one time. He was adamant about saying no. I called him quite a few times. I kept calling people, not in a harsh way. I try to be as nice as I can, but I'm persistent.

He said to me, "Jimmy Smith. What don't you understand about the word no? I've said no to you at last 100 times. What don't you understand about that word?"

I said, "Phil, it's not what I don't understand about that word, it's what I understand about it. I spell the word K-N-O-W. You don't know enough to say no to me Phil. If you knew what I know, you would never say no."

I'm hardly alone in learning how to handle rejection. According to Richard Poe in *Wave 3: The New Era In Network Marketing*, while starting Amway, Richard DeVos and Jay Van Andel, America's 11th richest people, recruited 500 people. Of them, 495 dropped out. The five that didn't quit, built Amway. All $7 billion of Amway's business was built upon those five people. Jay and Rich simply worked through their numbers.

Bill Britt is one of the most successful distributors. Some years ago, *20/20* did a feature on Amway. They spent 19 minutes interviewing whiners and complainers—several distributors who had failed and showed the garages full of products they couldn't sell.

During the last minute of the show Mr. Britt was interviewed in front of his palatial home. He was asked, "Mr. Britt, this business has obviously worked for you. What is your secret?'

He replied, 'There is no secret. I simply showed the plan to 1,200 people. Nine hundred said no and only 300 signed up. Out of 300, only

85 did anything at all. Out of those 85, only 35 were serious and out of those 35, 11 made me millionaires."

Please Reject Me

Jimmy continued talking about a subject he knows better than just about anyone:

> Jason Boreyko, former cofounder of New Vision, told this story recently. When he was a distributor in Matol, he signed up 50 people. He heard a lot of nos on the way to those 50.
>
> Jason took one man he knew would be terrific in business to lunch, told him about the business and the man said no. Jason took the man to lunch again the next month and told him all the updates. Once again, the man said no.
>
> Jason sent him more information and took him to lunch again the next month and again the man said no. That went on for six months. The seventh month, something had changed for the man and he said yes. The individual made Jason over one million dollars.

QUICK STEPS: *COMMITMENT IS KEY.*

Your success is directly related to the degree which you're willing to work to find others like yourself who are committed to succeed. Would you be willing to go through 200 people to find the one who makes you $50,000 a month or to become a millionaire, or hear uncounted nos to sign up 50 people to find a million dollar person? I hope you will.

Follow Up

Persistence and follow up go hand in hand. When you receive rejections, keep coming back. Eventually, some of those who refused will agree.

As soon as you're rejected, approach someone else, but don't forget about the person who rejected you. Go back to him or her and try again.

When you find someone who can be a key to your success, stay in touch with him or her and keep following up.

When you follow up, try to keep your targets interested. Keep a record of each contact you made and how you approached him or her. The next time you make contact, vary your approach. Try to come up with something interesting so people will keep you on their radar screens. And if you keep at it for a while, they may eventually relent.

Jimmy Smith filled up a notebook with people he wanted to contact. He went through the process of calling everyone. He called and called and called. He kept following up. "The fortune is in the follow-up," Jimmy says. "In golf, in baseball, and in sports in general, it's the follow-through. In network marketing, it's the follow-up." Those who rise to the top, the top 1%, don't take no for an answer. They're persistent, relentless and consistently follow through.

Jimmy had a list of good networkers he had met over the years, so he called them. He gave product samples to them as gifts. Then he followed up—and he followed up time after time after time. Some took ten months, some took a year, some took ten years, but Jimmy stayed with it—he continued to follow up. He worked with them after they joined his downline. He led them, mentored them and supported them. Jimmy traveled to meetings and training sessions for them. He continually educated them.

Jimmy has a process that he followed persistently, tenaciously and it made him a success.

Keep calling until someone is definite, slams the door in your face and says, "Absolutely, no!"

Unless you're completely certain and don't have the slightest doubt, never give up. Keep trying. Find a way to get through, make your points and enlist them.

Sometimes you have to wait. Let time pass before you contact people again. Keeping at it is the path to success. For years a salesman knocked on

Wal-Mart's door without success. Then, suddenly something happened: Wal-Mart decided to make a change. Wal-Mart rewarded the salesman's perseverance by giving him an order that transformed his business and his life.

QUICK STEPS: *BE PERSISTENT.*

Persistence gets people to focus and give you their time and attention. The successful person may fall down seven times, but stay on his or her feet the eighth. Being persistent is a concept that must be ingrained in your mind. How often do you see your friends and associates quitting before they give themselves enough time to build momentum for their business? They see renowned artists, famous athletes and prosperous companies and rarely think about what it took for them to get to the top. Their success didn't just happen, it wasn't an accident and it didn't happen over night. It took hard work, time and persistence to reach their lofty heights.

Mark's Story

Mark Yarnell, a minister in a small town in Texas, was headed for bankruptcy. He was perilously close to losing his home and his car. When he looked for a way out, he discovered direct selling. He was also lucky to have a wise sponsor.

The sponsor promised Mark, "This business can set you free financially in one to three years. But to succeed, you will have to face and conquer four major enemies."

Mark agreed.

1. He began by inviting 200 friends to watch a video at his home. Eighty said, "No, not interested." Mark encountered Enemy #1, *rejection.*

2. "No problem," Mark said. "My sponsor warned me about that and I still have 120 people coming over." That was enemy #2, *deception.*

Mark deceived himself by thinking that 120 people would be interested.

3. "OK," Mark thought, "My sponsor warned me about deception two. 70 people came by to watch the tape, but 57 said that they were not interested. That was enemy #3, *apathy*.

4. Undaunted, Mark realized that 13 people signed up. However, 12 dropped out. Mark encountered enemy #4, *attrition*.

However, that one individual stuck it out, and that guy earns Mark more than $50,000 per month.

So do the math. Starting with 200 names, Mark found one star. From that small percentage, half of one percent, Mark found a rainmaker who brought in $600,000 for him annually.

Small percentages can create huge fortunes.

28
Compensation Plans

One of the best features of direct selling is how much money you can make. In fact, many people go into direct selling simply because they can make such big money.

Direct selling companies offer lucrative compensation plans, but these plans differ from company to company. At first glance, most may seem simple and straightforward, but when you delve into them more closely, they can be quite complex—infuriatingly complex.

Direct selling companies are just like any other type of business: they must make money to stay afloat. So they write compensation plans that are highly advantageous to them.

Their plans can be confusing, hard to understand and be filled with all sorts of baffling terms and conditions. Worse yet, they may not pay you as much as you thought you would receive.

WARNING: Before you sign on with a direct selling company, have a financial professional examine the company's compensation plan. Have your accountant or financial advisor carefully review the company's plan and explain it, point-by-point, to you. Make sure that you fully understand all terms and exactly how you will be paid. When it comes to compensation, you don't want any surprises!

Many network-marketing companies now exist and more are popping up each week. Since each company offers different compensation plans, it's impossible to outline them all. So I've decided to create two lists to help you evaluate various plans. The first is a list of important information on your status and relationship with a network-marketing company, and the second is a checklist of items to look for before you commit to joining any group.

Fact List

Before you sign on with a network-marketing group, understand the following:

1. You are not an employee of a direct selling company. The company does not withhold money from your compensation for taxes or benefits.

2. You are an independent contractor: a sales agent.

3. You get paid commissions on:

   a. What you sell

   b. What your downline sells

4. You earn by:

   a. Purchasing products wholesale and selling them retail

   b. Receiving commissions on products purchased or sold by your downline. These commissions are also called bonuses

5. You earn from your downline:

   a. The more distributors in your downline, the greater your sales volume

   b. You are paid not just on your distributors' sales, but on your distributor's distributors' sales for a certain number of levels or generations defined by your payment plan

   c. The percentage of commissions you're paid varies by the level defined in your company's compensation plan

6. You get paid only on your sales or on those of your downline:

a. You do not get paid on the sales of anyone above you—your upline or sponsors.

Checklist

In compensation plans, look for:

❑ Reasonable start-up costs. Try to keep your initial investment in the $100 to $500 range including product and distributor kit costs.

❑ Fast start bonuses—how soon can you earn them?

❑ Monthly minimum qualifications to become and remain a distributor. Ask how low is low?

❑ Whether the company has an automatic product-reordering system. An auto-ship system can be the key to a company's survival and your ongoing income.

❑ Merit and or performance based incentives and or bonuses. Good producers should be rewarded. Lazy or weak producers should not.

❑ No loss of your distributorship if you are inactive. You should only lose your distributorship if you sign off or don't meet required sales quotas.

❑ Established terms. Other than minor tweaks, compensation plans should not be subject to change by the company. If the terms can be easily changed, your earnings can arbitrarily be cut.

❑ Whether the amount of distributor commissions that are actually paid is within 35% to 55% of the company's revenue. A higher percentage of commission pay out by the company can sink it.

❑ Breakage, which are unearned commissions, go to the next qualified distributor, not back to the company.

❑ How payout plans are weighted. Are they:

a. Fast cash, which is front-loaded?

b. Job income replacement, which is middle-loaded?

❏ Whether the plan pays commission on one-shot purchases on products that are not fully paid for or on product vouchers that can be redeemed for products or services. If it does, it can distort the amount of products actually sold and commissions earned.

> Don't be confused if during the first month, you receive a check for a product you purchased. You will just be getting your money back, not getting a commission on the sale.

❏ A true asset. Look for a company that will keep paying you if you want to slow down or stop working.

❏ Whether your business can be inherited. Can you leave it to others and if so, are their any limits or restriction on whom?

❏ Can you incorporate your distributorship so others can work in your business and earn ownership?

Jimmy Says: I was never a great student, but I was always good with numbers. As a butcher, when I started out with my dad, a person would select a piece of meat, and you would weigh it and say "Two dollars and fifty cents." You had a bag, and you wrote "$2.50" on it. For each item a customer bought, you wrote the numbers: $2.50, $3.50, $4.50. Then when she was done, maybe 10 or 12 items, you would add all the numbers.

I got very good at adding them up, because I did it all the time. One day I decided, "Why don't I add it up in my head instead of writing it down and save time?" So I started adding the figures up in my head, but I'd round off everything to an even number, no pennies. Two-fifty, three dollars, you know.

So a lady would get 10 items, and I'd say, "That's ten dollars and fifty cents," or "Twelve dollars," and I got away with it for a while. Then my dad caught me and wanted to kill me. "You can't do that! You've got to write it down."

I said, "Okay, Dad, I'll write it down. I was just trying to save time."

Knowing math came in handy when I found out in network marketing that you could actually leverage yourself with people. I knew you could leverage yourself with real estate, stocks and bonds, investment money, and all that, but when I found out you could actually leverage yourself with people, I figured, "Wow, there's seven billion people in the world. You'll never run out of people, right?"

I learned the geometric progression of numbers. I always have my calculator handy; I'm always working the numbers. If you get five people working you, that's your team. Work with those five people, help them get five people apiece, and now you have 25 in your second level. If you teach your people well and they teach their people well, 25 will get five apiece, and you have 125 in your third level. If they get five, you have 625 in your fourth. They get five, and you have 3,125 in your fifth. They get five, and you have 15,625 in your sixth. They get five, and you have 78,125 in your seventh level.

I learned that only one company paid seven levels. So, I ended up with 97,000 people. If they all spend just $100 a month on product, the bonus volume, BV, which you get paid on, amounts to over nine million dollars. Nine million, seven hundred thousand dollars.

The average payout is five percent, so five percent of nine million dollars is $450,000 a month. Once those numbers added up in my brain, it was like a record playing in my head—*Think and Grow Rich.*

Now let's assume you have a ninety percent failure rate. That sounds high, but it's not unusual in this business. Yet if only one out of ten stayed in the business, ten percent of 97,000 is 9,700. If that many people spend $100 a month, that's $970,000. Five percent of that is $48,000 a month, or $12,000 a week.

I thought to myself, "I can fail ninety percent of the time and still make $48,000 a month." That's when I really got excited about the numbers.

You have to have a compensation that people can understand, so they can work it. Most compensation plans in the industry up till now were so convoluted you couldn't understand them, much less work them. I think they did that for a reason.

The Isagenix® compensation plan is only possible with supercomputers. You couldn't even imagine, couldn't conceive of our compensation plan without a supercomputer. I went from $5,000 a month at my first company to $5,000 a week at my second company to $5,000 a day at Isagenix®. With my family combined, we make over $15,000 a day. I'd say I'm going in the right direction."

Different direct selling companies have different compensation plans. The Isagenix® compensation plan, instead of putting everybody on the first level, puts people under people. You can only build two legs. You can only put two people in your first level.

If you sponsor four people, where do the next two go? Under the first two. If you sponsor 100 people, where do they go? They must go under the people that you've already put in, so you put them on to the left, one to the right, one to the left, one to the right. That creates teamwork, harmony, synergy and it's democracy. You are truly helping your people.

It' a level playing field for everybody. The person that comes in today gets treated exactly like the first one was treated. Jimmy Smith gets no special treatment. One person is sponsored to his right, one to his left. They're active; he's active, spending $100 a month. Each person is paid 6% of the entire amount.

The person that signs up today gets the same deal. As soon as they sponsor one person right and one person left, they get 6% of their entire team's bonus volume. That's a fair plan, benefiting everybody equally.

29
Summing Up

Let's go back to where we started and review what you have learned.

Because of the speed of information, the Internet, mobile phones and other communication devices along with global competition, you have to bring valuable solutions to your customers—or someone else will. But with some much competition, it is difficult to rise above the static. Everyone in your related business claims the same benefits and features. Your customers are overwhelmed and confused by the endless messages.

Few people succeed in any business, and direct selling is no different. Direct selling is a way to make money or a type of business model. Other business models are traditional small businesses, larger businesses and franchises. Each business model requires certain investments of capital and certain risks.

What I have shown you is that in the Performance Economy, we are all in the entertainment business. In some sense, we all have shows, producers, directors, scripts, actors and a host of others to put on our show.

In the direct selling business model, you have a small up-front investment and a blueprint to do business given to you by the direct selling company and supported by your sponsors in your upline.

For all the support and infrastructure the direct selling company gives you, you get a small percentage of the revenue in the form of a mark-up to customers or a small sales commission.

You don't own any part of the network-marketing company. You are an independent contractor—your own boss.

To succeed in direct selling, you have to build directly and indirectly a large downline. There are no shortcuts. You can use Jimmy's strategy and find five superstars. You can use the Internet and other tools and methods I have outlined to get beyond your warm list and reach many more people than you could have in the past.

There is no substitute for hard, smart work that embraces the multiple-strategy approach I am recommending. Doing what everyone else is doing will get you where most are—earning little or no money in direct selling.

Is network marketing a pyramid scheme? As Jimmy explained, yes, network marketing companies have pyramid structures just like most every business out there, but not all network marketing companies are pyramid scams. Certain companies sell the quick-hit get-rich-quick approach, which the numbers on paper make seem so simple to reach.

There are some great companies out there but not near the amount that are vying for you to join.

I would stick with the more seasoned companies that have a proven track record.

Is there an advantage to getting in on the ground floor? Sure. But it's a crap shoot since so many network-marketing companies fail in the first year.

The excitement of direct selling is the close parallel to social networking and other forms of social media. If you can combine these worlds, you can succeed potentially beyond your wildest dreams.

That is Jimmy's belief. Jimmy is an inspiration to anyone who is feeling old. He is also a role model for anyone who believes that hard work and persistence leads to being in that elite group: the richest 1% in the world.

Good luck, and let me know how you are progressing!

Appendix 1
Gary's Home Office Organizing Tips

I've designed my home office in the following way to run multiple businesses with a fair amount of clarity and without too much clutter.

I have a large desk so I can have my computer, keyboard, speakers, mouse, and monitor in front of me with some space for legal pads, pen holders, and important letters and documents.

I found that I don't like desks with drawers because stuff just gets stuffed in them and it gets messy.

I have taken the file cabinets (two drawers fit legal size documents), and I have put them either in a closet or in the hall. I always have a couch that can roll out so that somebody can visit and sleep. I am very big on bookcases because I like to see all the books. They are organized by topic like you'd find in a bookstore. It is also stimulating and motivating to see all these great minds.

- **Phone System**

  A good phone system is a must. I have at least two lines—a third line is call waiting. Very important is lighting. I have lamps and overhead lighting for various places so I can move around and still read or work.

- **Supplies**

  On an as needed basis, I get them from Staples, Office Depot or Office Max.

- **Computers**

  Very important: I have back up systems for my computer. I also have people who are on call if my computers go down. That is a big area because if you don't get the right people they are just going to take you to the cleaners. Really make sure their pricing is competitive and they are really competent. If things are always going down, they are incompetent or creating work for themselves.

- **Extension Cords**

  I use a lot of extension cords so I can have a lot of electrical devices that are supportive.

- **Recording Machines**

  I have recording machines now so if I go someplace I can record. I have my cell phone and computer.

Decor

I dress up my office with some paintings and framed photos of my family.

- **Presentations**

  I also have an easel on a tripod so when I have meetings, I or others can sketch things out and brainstorm easily. I use with these easels large paper pads such as Post IT (2.5 feet x 2.5 feet or 5.2^2 feet) that I can clip to the easel. I can detach the paper and stick it up on the wall.

- **Video**

  I have a flip camera and a video camera. Basically, I have set myself up as a multimedia publishing company so that I can get things out in different formats.

- **Teamwork**

I have different teams that help me edit. I have outside editors and inside editors. My daughter Danielle works as an in-house editor. My other daughter Alexandra works in overseeing the administrative details as well as making sure our technologies are working such as our website.

I have a whole team of people working on different aspects of the company while I focus on keeping the vision and executing our business plan and business models.

- **Education**

  I love educating myself and others. I set my goals and my rewards as well as ask others to do the same for the company and for themselves.

- **Calendar**

  We use Google calendar to keep track of people and the key appointments or deadlines or rewards such as a good dinner, a vacation or exciting upcoming event.

Accounting

I use QuickBooks. You need to have a system in place so that you can either do your books yourself or have a bookkeeper do them for you. Either way, you want to input all your financial activities into a program such as QuickBooks.

Appendix 2
Important Financial and Accounting Terms

Assets - Liabilities = Net Worth

Remember that an asset puts money in your pocket whether you work for it or not, such as a bond or a dividend paying stock.

Assets are reflected on your balance sheet. Your balance sheet is a snapshot of your business on a given day. Your balance sheet shows you your assets such as cash and accounts receivable. It also shows your liabilities or that which takes money out of your pocket, such as a bank loan or a mortgage. The difference between your assets and liabilities is your net worth.

Revenues - Expenses = Profits (or Losses)

Revenues are the income you bring in to your company whether you collect them immediately or someone promises to pay you for your product or services within a period of time (these become on your balance sheet your accounts receivable).

Expenses are what you pay out or promise to pay out which relate to your revenues. The difference between your revenues and your expenses is your profit (+) or loss (-).

Balance Sheets and Income Statements

As noted, your balance sheet reflects the position of your company on a given day, i.e., its assets and liabilities.

Your income statement reflects your revenues and expenses between two periods of time.

Picture your balance sheet as a static or non-flow statement since it records where you are on a certain day.

Picture your income statement as a dynamic or flow statement, since it is recording the movement of revenues and expenses between two dates and time. For example, you might want to record your weekly revenues and expenses from Monday through Sunday of a certain week. Or, you might want to record your revenues and expenses for each month such as January, February etc.

Appendix 3
Outside Support Team

Accountant

One of the key lessons I learned was always to have an excellent accountant. Accountants—not bookkeepers—really frame your finances and tax status. A good accountant can save you much more than you pay them.

Lawyer

At times you will need a lawyer. Over the years I have developed enough skill to write basic business contracts. I went to law school one year, and this gave me some insight into the law. However, for any meaningful document, especially with any degree of complexity, I most definitely would use a top attorney.

Tech Team

In this age of the Internet, mobile phones and technology you need to find the best people to outline your technology needs and make sure that these technologies are working to your advantage. Technology is where you get the ultimate leverage in being able to reach people fast and efficiently. Go get my free special report called "Mastering the Art of Leverage." Here's the link: **http://www.masteringtheartofleverage.com/**

Appendix 4
Closing Techniques

Jimmy Smith is a master at closing, and he has a variety of techniques that really work. Every company has them, so make sure you master them before you made your first call. Let's see what Jimmy considers the best ways to close the deal:

Check Closes

These are subtle closes that you will constantly use throughout your presentation. (Find out if they are accepting what you are saying.) Example: "Doesn't it make sense that if our products are the best and they're priced competitively, that we will capture some reasonable market shares of these huge billion dollar markets?" (If you're talking to your prospect in person, nod your head yes.)

Assumption or Power of Suggestion Closes

This is when you just assume they will sponsor in and say, "Let's get you started" or "I assume you're ready to get started" or "When you go home tonight and try these products you will see how great they are."

Alternate Choice Closes

This is the most common close that you will want to use. This is when you give your prospect more than one choice, but either answer is acceptable to you.

Examples:

1. Is Thursday or Friday better to get together?

2. Is Monday morning good or is Tuesday afternoon better?

3. After a presentation, stay seated and look at your prospect and say, "That's the story about our company. Do you have any questions?" Answer any questions and then say, "Give me your honest opinion, are these products you would like to use?" Or "Is this a business you would like to build by becoming one of our distributors?"

Miscellaneous Closes

1. "If everything you have been told is true, what would stop you from getting started?"

2. "Now that you have seen the website, what else do you need to know before you get started?"

3. "So, what else do you need to know before you get started?"

The Jimmy Smith Close

"I have room to help one, maybe two more people. I'm looking to commit to helping someone achieve all their goals and dreams, but I've learned in order for me to do that, you must also commit a few things to me.

1. You must make an unconditional one-year commitment to do whatever it takes.

2. You must be willing to handle all obstacles and challenges that come your way.

3. You must be coachable.

4. You must come to all weekly meetings and monthly trainings for the next year.

5. You must be willing to write down all of your goals.

If you are ready to make that commitment, I will get you started. If you would like to think about it, that's fine. What would you like to do?"

Remember, if your prospect is not interested in becoming a distributor, you can retail products to them and ask for referrals.

Here is a vitally important point: After each question, be quiet and wait for an answer. Let them make the choice. They have to own the decision if they're really going to become part of your downline.

Give your prospects your best support as they become set up.

That's the key to success in direct selling: helping other people. When you sponsor somebody into this business, the word "sponsor" means to take responsibility for their success.

When you sponsor someone, you have to tell him, "This is not get rich quick. You have to be willing to spend some time and some sweat equity. You have to do this with a passion. If you do it timidly, by putting your toe in the water, and saying, "Maybe I will and maybe I won't," then guess what? "Maybe I will and maybe I won't" doesn't work. You have to be passionate. You have to give it everything you have. You have to want this more than anything else in the world. When you feel that way, when you act that way, then alone will you be successful. Half measures will avail you of absolutely nothing in this venture or any other venture.

BUY A SHARE OF THE FUTURE IN YOUR COMMUNITY

These certificates make great holiday, graduation and birthday gifts that can be personalized with the recipient's name. The cost of one S.H.A.R.E. or one square foot is $54.17. The personalized certificate is suitable for framing and will state the number of shares purchased and the amount of each share, as well as the recipient's name. The home that you participate in "building" will last for many years and will continue to grow in value.

Here is a sample SHARE certificate:

YES, I WOULD LIKE TO HELP!

I support the work that Habitat for Humanity does and I want to be part of the excitement! As a donor, I will receive periodic updates on your construction activities but, more importantly, I know my gift will help a family in our community realize the dream of homeownership. **I would like to SHARE in your efforts against substandard housing in my community!** *(Please print below)*

PLEASE SEND ME _____ SHARES at $54.17 EACH = $ $_____

In Honor Of: _____

Occasion: *(Circle One)*   HOLIDAY   BIRTHDAY   ANNIVERSARY

OTHER: _____

Address of Recipient: _____

Gift From: _____ *Donor Address:* _____

Donor Email: _____

I AM ENCLOSING A CHECK FOR $ $_____ PAYABLE TO HABITAT FOR HUMANITY OR PLEASE CHARGE MY VISA OR MASTERCARD *(CIRCLE ONE)*

Card Number _____ Expiration Date: _____

Name as it appears on Credit Card _____ Charge Amount $ _____

Signature _____

Billing Address _____

Telephone # Day _____ Eve _____

PLEASE NOTE: Your contribution is tax-deductible to the fullest extent allowed by law.
Habitat for Humanity • P.O. Box 1443 • Newport News, VA 23601 • 757-596-5553
www.HelpHabitatforHumanity.org